scm centrebooks : *six christians*

David Anderson

Simone Weil

SCM PRESS LTD

334 01756 4

First Published 1971
by SCM Press Ltd
56 Bloomsbury Street London

© *SCM Press Ltd 1971*

Printed in Great Britain by
Billing & Sons Limited
Guildford and London

For Helen, Margaret,
Christine and Jeremy

Contents

Acknowledgments

The extracts from *Waiting on God* are quoted by permission of Routledge & Kegan Paul Ltd, and the quotation from T. S. Eliot's *Four Quartets* by permission of Faber & Faber Ltd.

Preface

When I was planning this book, I thought I would have to
go to France to consult some of those who had known
Simone Weil and to look up various documents about her.
This had its attractions, but it turned out to be unnecessary.
The 'leg-work' had already been done by Jacques Cabaud,
whose detailed biography of Simone Weil appeared in
French in 1957 and in an amplified English version in 1964
under the title, *Simone Weil: A Fellowship in Love*. To
Cabaud's book I am greatly indebted for much biographical
material which has not appeared elsewhere. I have also
made use of a number of other biographies in French and
English to which reference is made in the bibliography.
Consultation of books by and about Simone Weil has been
made easy for me by the excellent library of Maison
Française, Oxford.

English readers of Simone Weil owe a great deal to
Sir Richard Rees, not only for his own perceptive book
about her, but also for his translation and editing of many
of Simone Weil's writings. I was glad to learn from him
that he has translated *La Connaissance surnaturelle*, and
that this important work, together with some hitherto
unpublished notes from the earlier period of Simone's life,
is to be published by OUP later this year under the title
First and Last Notebooks.

Various people have written to me expressing interest in
Simone Weil and, in some cases, mentioning their own

study of her work. She seems to be becoming a popular choice for PhD theses, and certainly it would be hard to find a more rewarding one.

Inevitably, a book like this must cover some ground already traversed by others, but I have also tried to include material which has received rather less attention. So far as I know, my exposition of Simone's analogy of the geometric mean in chapter 8 has not been done before. As I have said, she was a great crosser of boundaries, and some of her most fascinating ideas are to be found in her comparisons and correlations.

I never met Simone Weil, though I happened to be doing an Army Intelligence course in London in 1942-3 when she was working for the Free French. I like to think that I may, unknowingly, have sat beside her at a National Gallery concert or rubbed shoulders with her in the crowd at Speakers' Corner.

Oxford, 1970

Bibliography

Books by Simone Weil, with abbreviations used in text

CO   *La Condition ouvrière*, Gallimard, Paris 1951

CS   *La Connaissance surnaturelle*, Gallimard, Paris 1950

EHP   *Ecrits historiques et politiques*, Gallimard, Paris 1960

GG   *Gravity and Grace*, Routledge & Kegan Paul (paperback) 1963

IC   *Intimations of Christianity*, Routledge & Kegan Paul 1957

NR   *The Need for Roots*, Routledge & Kegan Paul 1952

OL   *Oppression et Liberté*, Gallimard, Paris 1955

P   *Poèmes* (including *Venise sauvée*), Gallimard, Paris 1968

SE   *Selected Essays, 1934–43*, OUP 1962

SG   *La Source grecque*, Gallimard, Paris 1953

SL   *Seventy Letters*, OUP 1965

SNLG   *On Science, Necessity and the Love of God*, OUP 1968

WG   *Waiting on God*, Collins Fontana 1959

Books about Simone Weil

ARG   Anne Reynaud-Guérithault, *Simone Weil: Leçons de philosophie*, Plon, Paris 1959

CM   Charles Moeller, *Littérature du XXe siècle et christianisme*, tome I, Casterman, Paris 1957

EWFT   E. W. F. Tomlin, *Simone Weil*, Bowes & Bowes 1954

GT   G. Thibon, Preface to *Gravity and Grace*, Routledge & Kegan Paul (paperback) 1963

JC   Jacques Cabaud, *Simone Weil: A Fellowship in Love*, Harville Press 1964

JMP   J. M. Perrin, Introduction to *Attente de Dieu*, La Colombe, Paris 1950

MMD   Marie-Magdeleine Davy, *Simone Weil*, Editions Universitaires, Paris 1956

PT   J. M. Perrin and G. Thibon, *Simone Weil as We Knew Her*, Routledge & Kegan Paul 1953

RR   Richard Rees, *Simone Weil, A Sketch for a Portrait*, OUP 1966

1 Introduction

The year before she died, Simone Weil wrote to her friend Father Perrin a letter in which she explained why she did not feel able to accept baptism into the Roman Catholic church. Among her reasons she included the following:

> Christianity should contain all vocations without exception since it is catholic. In consequence the church should also. But in my eyes Christianity is catholic by right but not in fact. So many things are outside it, so many things that I love and do not want to give up, so many things that God loves, otherwise they would not be in existence.[1]

Unlike most of us, in our more or less settled orthodoxies, Simone Weil wanted to touch life at as many points as possible. She was one of those extremely rare people to whom the familiar words of Terence can justly be applied: 'I am a human being, and I count nothing human as alien to me.' She was a professional teacher of philosophy and she had immense erudition, but her awareness of life was never that of a remote intellectual brooding over ideas in an academic solitude. Whenever possible, she sought out opportunities for sharing in the physical toil of manual workers, and she once remarked upon the lack of such experience among the self-appointed political champions of the working class. Her health was never good, but there can be little doubt that her death at the age of thirty-four was partly caused by an accumulated exhaustion resulting from her work in factories and on the land. She told Father

Perrin that nothing gave her more pain than the idea of separating herself from the immense and unfortunate multitude of unbelievers. She believed that she had the vocation 'to move among men of every class and complexion' in order to know them and 'to love them just as they are'. It was because she felt that membership of the church would diminish this total awareness and enclose her in a narrow security that she refused baptism.

In the later years of her short life Simone Weil reached a level of mystical speculation which may well place her among the greatest religious thinkers of this or any age; yet during that period her dearest wish was to join the French Resistance and to be given the most dangerous jobs. She believed that she would be able to withstand torture better than most and was confident that she would not give away secrets if she were captured. This was no mere bravado. For much of her life she had suffered from excruciating headaches, but she had learned, as she said, to gather together all her pain into a small point and then to set it aside. Pain had become part of what she called *malheur* – by which she meant affliction of such desolating intensity that the self is 'pulverized' and the soul becomes accessible to God. The willing acceptance of the pains of the flesh and of the harsh, cold, brutal 'necessity' of the world was for Simone Weil one of the chief ways to the silent presence of the divine reality. But her mysticism was never a flight from reality here below into a wholly other reality above. It was true that the 'necessity' of the world was separated by an infinite distance from the goodness of God, but redemption consisted precisely in the harmonization of contraries, in the attainment to that state of the soul in which suffering and glory become one and the vertical and horizontal dimensions of awareness intersect. Simone Weil had an unmitigated horror of anything that could be called 'escapism'. The kind of religion which is merely a consolation for the anguish of human existence was not only alien to her own deepest experience; she was convinced that it was a certain way of putting the divine reality out of one's reach for ever. She abhorred equally the kind of life which is sealed off from the transcendent and the kind of life which seeks a solitary exaltation unpenetrated by the affliction of the world. Her own life was an astonishing combination of both intensities. And the point at which those intensities met was the cross of Christ.

Simone Weil's cast of mind made any dogmatic exclusivism impossible for her. She believed that the authentic Christian vision had been present in the cultures of ancient Egypt and Greece and in the teaching of Hinduism. She thought that the vision had been more faithfully preserved in some of the Christian heresies than in orthodox Catholicism, and she viewed the history of the church from the time of its recognition as the State religion of the Roman Empire as a record of increasing compromise with collective power, backed up by the use of anathemas to eliminate opposition. It seemed to Simone Weil that the church had used dogma as a weapon in the service of political ambition, with the result that its life had become further and further removed from the ideals of the gospel. The freedom of speculative, individual intelligence had been stifled, and the authentic, universal vision of early Christianity had become darkened. Although the church had the duty to guard against error, that did not include the right to excommunicate those who fell into it, and the use of the words *anathema sit* seemed to Simone Weil to be an absolute denial of the openness of Christianity to the world.

As other mystical writers had done before her, Simone Weil distinguished between two kinds of religious language – the collective and the individual. The collective language is the language of public doctrinal formulation which the church teaches as its rule of faith; the individual language is the language of the soul's personal intercourse with God, words which are heard 'in secret amidst the silence of the union of love'. When the two languages are in disagreement, that is simply due to the fact that 'the language of the market place is not that of the nuptial chamber'.[2]

We may agree with Simone Weil that it is necessary to make some distinction between public and private theological language.[3] Difficulty arises, however, when the private language of mystical contemplation is offered as, or is mistaken for, the public language of doctrinal statement. It is, for example, easy to accuse Simone Weil of denying the uniqueness of Christ and of distorting Christian belief by accommodating it to pagan and gnostic types of speculation. Some of her writing suggests a mind which was almost perverse in its admiration of pre-Christian thought, and it is probably true to say that her pre-formed loves and hatreds led her into some grotesque errors of historical judgment. Everything was categorized according to the criterion of her own interior vision, and she had a strong tendency to cast into outer darkness whole movements of history which in her opinion failed to match that vision. Her style of writing was often oracular and uncompromising. She had little use for the nicely-calculated less or more which comes so easily to more casual minds. Simone Weil was decidedly not casual. She believed that, by the grace of God, she had been given a glimpse of truth, and she would willingly have died for it. In fact that is probably exactly what she did.

The result of Simone Weil's independence is that we learn more about the real values of life from her passions and prejudices than we do from the balanced statements of more temperate authorities. Men are not made to burn with desire for the Good by careful orthodoxy or reasonable compromise, but by the fire of a prophetic intelligence and vision.

Simone Weil was cast in the prophetic mould, but it would be wrong to give the impression that she was an impervious fanatic. She possessed something which is not always conspicuous among prophets, and that was a first-class intelligence. 'When the mysteries of faith are separated from all reason', she wrote, 'they are no longer mysteries but absurdities.'[4] Her range of knowledge was enormous and it included the sciences as well as the humanities. Her special training was in philosophy, yet she was capable of suggesting to her brother – a distinguished mathematician – a way of restating the Quantum Theory which, she believed, rendered unnecessary Planck's principle of discontinuity.[5] She was deeply interested in social and political theory and practice, and she wrote a number of essays on those subjects which subsequently gained the admiration of Albert Camus. Her excursions into history and literature, though they sometimes yielded bizarre results, indicate a formidable amount of reading and erudition. She once said that she did not read books, she *ate* them.

All this adds up to a somewhat daunting kind of figure. Few people found her easy to know, and Gustave Thibon tells us that, on first acquaintance, it was the less attractive side of her character that she displayed most readily. She was a tremendous talker at a high level of thought. Words poured from her in a rather flat tone of voice, leaving her hearers battered and exhausted. She seems to have been the kind of person who would talk about God at a garden-party, and the hearts of strong men must often have quailed when she hove into view. But few could fail to admire her.

There were some who got to know Simone Weil well enough to love her, and those who have recorded their impressions speak of her essential simplicity and greatness of soul. One of her pupils at the lycée in Roanne where Simone taught from 1933-4 has told us of the happy family feeling which developed in the philosophy class there and of the admiring affection in which the girls held their young teacher.[6] There are stories about Simone Weil's kindness to children. On holiday once she helped a fisherman's daughter to learn the catechism; on another occasion she helped a village boy with his arithmetic, and in London not long before she died she told nursery stories to her landlady's retarded son. One of her grandest obsessions was to introduce workers and peasants to the inheritance of culture. She was incapable of limiting herself to the privileged world of higher education in which, as an *agregée* of the Ecole Normal Supérieure, she had her recognized and rightful place, and she was prepared to take endless trouble with a mechanic or a village girl who seemed responsive to intellectual challenge. No doubt she often overestimated their capacity for learning and even made ludicrous psychological blunders in her assessment of them. There must have been many workers and peasants who escaped from her attentions with considerable relief. Yet her excesses were those of a great soul. To enlarge the awareness of workers beyond the mechanical servitude of their imprisoning labour seemed to Simone Weil to be a sacred duty. Her attitude was never a patronizing one – she had a profound hatred of all self-righteous condescension; rather, she believed that to be a human being is to be potentially capable of sharing in the totality of the human vision, and she viewed every form of élitism as a denial of our common humanity. Most of us pay lip-service to this idea and continue to hug our privileges. Simone Weil not only believed it, she also lived it.

Beneath Simone Weil's incessantly active intelligence,

there was, in her later years, a heart of silence where she 'waited on God'. Her closest friends increasingly recognized in her a level of awareness beyond their own. The material of her private speculations was for the most part confided to her notebooks which were not published until some years after her death. They contain jottings and longer pieces which are rather similar in form to the *Pensées* of Pascal, and the volume entitled *La Connaissance surnaturelle* opens with an account of what seems to have been a deeply mystical experience. The notebooks reveal an extension of the lines of her earlier political and philosophical thought into a more definitively religious area of experience and speculation, but they do not suggest any real discontinuity between the two stages of her development. Although Christ did not 'come down' and 'take possession' of her until she was about thirty, it cannot be supposed that she underwent a totally unexpected 'conversion'. Perhaps we may say that she had already known Christ as present in the poor and afflicted to whom she had dedicated her life. Simone believed that human experience contained what she called 'forms of the implicit love of God', and the first of those forms was love of neighbour. When Christ came to her 'in person', she must have recognized in him a known and already welcomed friend.

NOTES

1. WG p. 41.
2. WG p. 45.
3. One of the earliest theologians to do this was Dionysius the Areopagite (*c.* AD 500), who distinguished between 'apophatic' or mystical theology and 'kataphatic' or rational theology.
4. CS p. 56.
5. SL pp. 134–5.
6. ARG Introduction.

2   Child, Student and Teacher

Simone Weil was born in Paris on 3 February 1909. Her father, Bernard Weil, was a doctor. The family lived first in the Boulevard de Strasbourg and then in the Boulevard St Michel – the famous street which runs through the heart of the Latin Quarter, lined with cafés and bookshops where students of the University of Paris discuss affairs and make plans to astound the bourgeois. Simone grew up in an atmosphere of culture and scepticism. Her parents were Jewish but they were agnostic and Simone herself put 'the question of God's existence' to one side – until the time came when it refused to stay there any longer.

Early photographs of Simone at the age of two and six reveal her as a rather serious-looking girl with good features, dark eyes, and an unruly mop of very black hair. A later photograph taken when she was thirteen shows her smiling attractively, with her hair fluffed out on either side of her face. A studio portrait shows how good-looking she was, but gives her an improbable air of sultry glamour.[1] Simone soon gave up caring about her appearance. Bad eyesight obliged her to wear glasses and she preferred a plain simplicity of dress which did nothing to enhance her looks. She passed through the normal emotional crises of adolescence, but even at that time her interests were intellectual rather than romantic. She said later that, although she had been tempted to try to get to know love, she had decided not to – in order to avoid committing herself before she was mature enough to know what she wished from life.[2]

Although Simone's abilities as a child were exceptional by any ordinary standards, she felt that she was over-shadowed by her brother André, three years older than herself, whose childhood, as she said later, was comparable in brilliance to that of Pascal. Simone despaired of ever being more than second-rate, but in fact brother and sister seem to have been closer to each other than she realized. Both were studious and took little interest in sport. Jacques Cabaud tells us that a lady was once greatly put out by their incessant conversation on a tram, remarking that the children had been brought up like parrots.[3]

Simone's schooling had been interrupted by the war, but when the Weils returned to Paris she went first to the lycée Fenelon and then to the lycée Victor Duruy where she did a year's philosophy and obtained her baccalauréat in 1925. She was an able pupil and was admitted to the lycée Henri IV where she entered the philosophy class presided over by Emile Chartier, better known by his pseudonym Alain.

Alain was a teacher of genius. Perhaps he was not a thinker of marked originality (one of his colleagues referred to him as a 'tapestry-weaver'), but he had the gift of ex-pounding the great philosophers, especially Plato, Descartes and Kant, in a way which his students never forgot. André Maurois has recently described the admiration and affection which Alain inspired. As an old man he still welcomed his former pupils with unfailing courtesy and interest. When Maurois gave the oration at Alain's funeral, he said, 'Socrates is not dead, he lives in Plato. Plato is not dead, he lives in Alain. Alain is not dead, he lives in us.'[4] Few teachers have received a comparable tribute, though perhaps it was not shared by all of Alain's pupils. Jean-Paul Sartre's existentialism was in some respects a reaction against the more assured metaphysics of his former master, who seems

21

to have been a stranger to the anxiety of existence which Sartre has made his major concern.

Simone Weil came under Alain's spell and acquired from him a devotion to the Greek philosophers (except Aristotle whom she disliked because he argued in favour of slavery) which she kept for the rest of her life. But Simone's temperament was very different from that of Alain. He was a philosopher in the classical French tradition – urbane, detached, sceptical and agnostic. But Simone was already a philosopher of passion whose thought tended towards extremes and whose mind could be content with nothing less than absolute truth. She seems to have tried hard to conceal her inner conflicts from her fellow-students, and she imitated Alain's debunking style in a flat, monotonous tone of voice which was, no doubt, partly an affectation. Her manner was brittle and her lack of interest in feminine intimacies and student romance caused her to be regarded as an eccentric individualist. Her independence of mind and her rejection of intellectual compromise did not easily blend with the prevailing ideal of detached, sceptical inquiry. It is probable that Alain's chief contribution to Simone Weil's development was to introduce her to the writings of his own teacher Jules Lagneau, a man who had known the kind of metaphysical 'affliction' which was already stirring in the soul of Simone Weil. 'Certitude', he wrote, 'is an absolute creation of the spirit; it is the spirit itself, it is the absolute, it is God who creates it in us.'[5] Some of Simone Weil's later religious writing could almost be said to be a commentary on that text.

In 1927 Simone failed the entrance examination to the École Normale Supérieure. Like many students before and since, she had worked at the subjects which interested her (philosophy and mathematics) and had neglected the rest. She also admitted that she had spent too much time in cafés. The failure was a salutary one, and the following year, in spite of an illness in March, she sat again and passed. Simone was placed first in the list of entrants, with Simone de Beauvoir (the novelist) second.

The Ecole Normale Supérieure of Paris is the most prestigious of all French institutions of higher education. In Simone Weil's time, it had only recently begun to admit women students. It is, as the name indicates, a college for future teachers, and its students must undertake to teach for at least ten years after qualifying. The standards of the Ecole are very high. In the earlier years of its existence, it was run on lines which were virtually indistinguishable from those of a monastery. The hour of rising was 5 a.m., though a concession to the weakness of student flesh was made on Mondays and Fridays when a lie-in until 6 a.m. was permitted. Although this early asceticism has been abated in modern times (one cannot easily picture its enforcement today), the Ecole is still severe in its intellectual and academic requirements. Many students have in the past failed to qualify, and those who do qualify are reckoned, by themselves at least, as the educational élite of the country. Some of the most famous names in modern French literature, philosophy and politics are those of former students of the ENS.

To a person as gifted as Simone Weil, the Ecole Normale held no terrors. She specialized in philosophy and continued to attend Alain's classes at the lycée Henri IV, as did many of his former pupils. Simone submitted articles to him for publication in his periodical *Libres Propos*. Her first published piece was a somewhat obscure treatise on the nature of manual work – a subject which later became one of her dedicated concerns. She was attracted to Marxism, and many people took her for a communist though she never became one. She rapidly developed interests and activities

23

outside the curriculum of the Ecole Normale. The most significant of these was perhaps her involvement in teaching at a college for railway workers (something like the French equivalent of our WEA) to which she gave herself with great enthusiasm. Her commitment to trade-unionism and to the education of workers was to continue for the rest of her life, and led her to a determination to experience manual work at first-hand in factories and on the land. Her first taste of this occurred when she was on holiday in Normandy and helped to bring in the harvest. She suffered from headaches and had little stamina, but she forced herself to work as hard as the men. She was and continued to be a person of inflexible determination and courage, often pushing herself beyond the limits of her physical endurance. One of the farm workers in Normandy said that Joan of Arc must have been like Simone Weil.

The impression one gains of Simone Weil at this period is of a not altogether attractive person whom it must have been hard to ignore. What seems to stand out most is her personal integrity and her increasing dedication to the vocation which she was already beginning to make her own. She continued to admire Alain, but she asserted her own views with such unconditioned assurance that she was nicknamed 'the Categorical Imperative in skirts'.[6] Her political leanings were left-wing and pacifist. There was, of course, nothing remarkable about that in itself. Many students enjoy a flirtation with the political left, and there are some who even manage to persuade themselves that they have repudiated bourgeois values; moreover, the pacifist attitude was normal between the wars (in England, we may recall the activities of the Peace-Pledge Union, and the Oxford Union's refusal to fight for king and country). But what distinguished Simone Weil from most other students was the persistent passion of her convictions and the determination with which she sought to live by them. She seems to have been genuinely ashamed of her bourgeois privileges and her comfortable home. She was capable of feeling deep distress for the sufferings of Chinese children, and stories are told of her withering remarks to fellow students who seemed to be bearing the afflictions of others with excessive fortitude. Perhaps Simone had more than her share of the unaccommodating certitude of youth, and in a sense she never lost it. Once her own position was determined, it became unshakable. Father Perrin, who knew her towards the end of her life, tells us that he does not remember a single instance when Simone yielded to argument. This characteristic was already evident in her student days. It is not hard to guess which side of the barricades she would have been on had she been a student in May 1968.

Her personal appearance did little to make her attractive. She took no interest in it, though she had pretty hair and a good complexion. No doubt the headaches which never left her for long made it difficult for her to admire her own body, but it seems likely that her plainness of dress was a kind of 'uniform' of her vocation, separating her off from middle-class status. She smoked heavily and rolled her own cigarettes (rather unskilfully). This was probably for reasons of economy, though one may guess that it was also for Simone a mark of her solidarity with the proletariat. She was a bizarre character, even by the standards of the Ecole Normale.

Simone's pacifism was expressed through her association with a student protest against conscription. Male students of the Ecole Normale automatically received commissions in the army, and there were some who thought that recruitment should be voluntary rather than compulsory. An antimilitarist petition was drawn up for presentation to the director of the Ecole, and Simone Weil was one of its most vocal advocates. The director, Bouglé, rejected the petition and referred to Simone Weil as 'The Red Virgin'. Like many of those who were students in the 1920s and 30s, Simone continued to be a convinced pacifist until Hitler's territorial claims made the pacifist position untenable.

It must have been with some feeling of relief that the faculty of the Ecole welcomed Simone's graduation. The director is reported as having said that she would be given a post as far away from Paris as possible. Much against her own wishes (she wanted to work in an industrial area or a sea-port) she was appointed to the girls' lycée of a small town called Le Puy, and her application for the lycée of Valenciennes was turned down. The final report in her dossier referred to her as 'a brilliant student' and commented on her wide range of knowledge not only in philosophy but also in literature and contemporary art. Out of a hundred and seven successful candidates, she was placed seventh along with eleven others. She had not been wasting her time.

In 1931, after a holiday with her parents on the coast of Normandy where, characteristically, she worked with the fishermen, Simone packed her bags and departed for her first teaching post at the girls' lycée of Le Puy. Her job was to teach philosophy to senior girls preparing for university entrance. The girls quickly recognized her as an original. No doubt they expected something unusual in a brilliant graduate of the Ecole Normale, and they were not disappointed. Simone had few of the accepted teaching skills. She peered myopically at her papers instead of looking at the class, and her physical clumsiness made her use of the blackboard a hazardous entertainment. Her voice was low and monotonous, her appearance neat but extremely plain. It says much for the seriousness of the pupils that she seems to have had no problems of discipline.

26

The truth is, however, that these intelligent girls were quick to respond to an exceptional mind. Simone's rather tedious delivery did not conceal her range of learning or her love of intellectual adventure. She treated her pupils as equals, seeking to awaken in them a response to great ideas rather than to cram them for examinations. Her methods were open to criticism by her superiors, who looked for solid academic results rather than diffuse Socratic inquiries, but Simone Weil seems to have been ahead of her time in her way of encouraging free and creative thinking. As might be expected, her best pupils gained much from this treatment, but examination results were disappointing.

A letter written by Simone Weil to a colleague about this time describes her way of teaching 'Method in the Sciences'. She remarks that her pupils regarded the sciences as compilations of cut-and-dried knowledge, without having any idea of the connections between them or of the methods by which they were created. Simone had offered some extra classes on the history of science which all the girls had attended voluntarily. She had given them 'a rapid sketch' of the development of mathematics, from the discovery of the properties of similar triangles, through the arithmetic theory of Pythagoras to the discovery of incommensurables and the geometric theory of proportion discovered by Eudoxus. This led on to modern geometry, algebra and the calculus, and to the application of mathematics to physics which the calculus made possible. All this, Simone reported, was followed by the pupils 'with passionate interest' even on the part of 'those most ignorant in science'.[7]

This letter is particularly revealing of Simone Weil's own intellectual interests. She was later to make considerable use of Greek science in the exposition of her philosophical and theological ideas. The foundations of this had

27

evidently been laid at an early stage, and no doubt the 'passionate interest' displayed by her pupils was a reflection of that of their teacher. Indeed, the notes taken by one of Simone's pupils at Roanne (where Simone taught from 1933–4)[8] show that many of the ideas contained in her mature writings were firmly settled in her mind well before she developed them in the light of her religious experience. This suggests that Simone Weil's religion had more to do with the natural progress of her thought than with some kind of unexpected 'conversion'.

There are, however, only a few references to religion in Simone's published class notes.[9] The subject came up in connection with moral philosophy, when Simone discussed the possibility of basing moral imperatives on the will of God. She argued that this doctrine turned God into a kind of gendarme and emptied moral obedience of its virtue. By definition, she said, since he is the supreme value God cannot be demonstrated, and those who believe that they come into contact with God by mystical experience commit a kind of blasphemy.[10] Simone Weil was to retain this doctrine of the transcendent otherness of God, but she was to discover that, by a sort of 'miracle', the transcendent God could be known.

Simone worked hard as a teacher of philosophy and seems to have taken a deep personal interest in her pupils (she sometimes invited them to accompany her on walking holidays). But she would not have been herself if she had confined her activities to the lycée. We have seen that during her time at the Ecole Normale she had developed a deeply felt concern for the lot of the manual worker, and it is not surprising that she quickly became involved in politics and trade-unionism at Le Puy and elsewhere.

For a number of reasons, the full force of the economic depression of the early 1930s did not reach France until

1934, but even so there was enough unemployment in 1931 to cause considerable unrest. The trade-union movement was split by rivalry between communists and socialists, with the result that it was impossible to present a united front to the employers, who were themselves facing the problem of declining markets. Simone allied herself with the workers and became an active supporter of the syndicalist movement associated with the journal 'La Revolution Prolétarienne' which was working for solidarity among the trade-unions. The centre of the movement in the Haute-Loire was the mining town of Saint-Etienne, and Simone soon paid a visit to its assistant secretary, a school teacher named Thévenon. She wrote a number of articles which reveal her whole-hearted support for Thévenon's ideas about unity. In one of them she said that the working class would have to solve the problem of unity or else condemn itself to atrophy as a revolutionary force. Thévenon and she collaborated in an education course for the miners in Saint-Etienne. This delighted Simone. She travelled from Le Puy each weekend and spent her extra allowance as an *agregée* on books for the library.

In Le Puy itself it was not long before Simone's political activities brought her notoriety. Her first brush with the authorities occurred when she headed a deputation of the unemployed to the mayor of Le Puy. The incident was reported in a provincial newspaper which made great play with the fact that Simone was a well-paid teacher, implying that her identification with the cause of the unemployed could not be other than bogus. No doubt it was thought that she would be discouraged by ridicule, but the authorities took her seriously and a police dossier was compiled and handed to the inspector of schools. Needless to say, Simone Weil could not be intimidated. She fraternized with workers in cafés, she walked about Le Puy with a copy of

29

the communist newspaper *l'Humanité* under her arm, and she continued to take a prominent part in deputations and demonstrations.

The next move of the authorities was to ban all demonstrations and processions in Le Puy. The unemployed therefore went to the labour exchange in small groups. One day, when they emerged from the building the police were waiting to search and question them. After this the men formed ranks and marched off in procession singing the Internationale. At the head was Simone Weil carrying a red flag.

A newspaper report of these events referred to Simone as 'a red virgin of the tribe of Levi, evangelist of the gospel of Moscow', and accused her of inciting the unemployed against the authorities.[11] But the campaign was now almost over. The unemployed were promised a benefit of 16 frs a day, feelings died down, and for the moment normality was restored.

Simone Weil, however, had by this time seriously compromised her position at the lycée and moves were made to have her transferred away from Le Puy. Many parents felt that it was undesirable that their daughters should be exposed to the influence of a teacher whose political views were notoriously of the extreme left, though the parents of Simone's own pupils had sent a petition to the minister of education pointing out that her teaching was impartial and adding that she had been a most valuable influence on the girls. But opposition grew, and, in spite of support for Simone on the part of some trade-unions, she was finally persuaded to sign an application for transfer. She may well have done this simply because she wanted a move to an industrial area where her activities would have greater scope!

These incidents at Le Puy illustrate both the strengths

and weaknesses of Simone's character. Her strength was her absolute dedication to the cause of the unemployed. It seemed to her scandalous that men should be unable to use their skills and were compelled to break stones for a pittance reluctantly doled out by the municipal authorities. Jacques Cabaud tells us that she shared so much of her salary with the unemployed that for a whole winter she went without heat, and her apartment was open at all hours so that men could go in and get some food.[12] All this was admirable and at an incomparably higher level of sacrifice than most of us would have been willing to occupy. Yet one also seems to detect in her an element of perverse extremism which in the end worked against the interests of her cause. Perhaps she went out of her way to shock the bourgeois citizens of Le Puy whose daughters had been entrusted to her, and one may suspect that she had an unconscious desire for martyrdom which was not entirely praiseworthy. She is said to have remarked that she had always regarded dismissal as the natural culmination of her career – words which were, of course, spoken in jest, but perhaps with an underlying hint of self-dramatization.

Simone Weil was widely taken for a communist, and she seems to have made no effort during her time in Le Puy to correct this mistake. We may be surprised that her political leanings should have caused so great a sense of outrage. Although communist parties have always had a hot and cold relationship with the intelligentsia, it was no uncommon thing in the 1930s for French intellectuals to be associated with the *Parti Communiste Française*, either as members or as fellow-travellers. After a number of convulsive purges in the late 1920s, the new secretary of the PCF, Maurice Thorez, had extended the hand of welcome to intellectuals and was gaining some distinguished recruits and supporters. But these men who joined or supported the party in the

1920s and 30s were nearly all either independent writers and journalists – we may think of Barbusse, Rolland, Aragon, Gide, Chamson, Malraux – or surrealist artists like Breton and Eluard.[13] Simone Weil, however, was an employee of the State, and as such she was expected to uphold the values of the social class to which she belonged. Her political activities could be represented as a betrayal of the society which gave her a living. Moreover, the normal and acceptable contribution of intellectuals to the class conflict was by way of their skill as writers or artists. They were not expected to lead processions of workers carrying a red flag as Simone Weil had done. After her heady experience at Le Puy, Simone herself turned more towards the traditional role of the political intellectual and busied herself with writing, though without giving up her right to demonstrate when occasion required. As we shall see, her articles were not of a kind to please the PCF, and she came to regard all political parties as incarnations of collectivism and self-interest.

At the end of the academic year 1932, Simone Weil left Le Puy, and one can imagine that some sighs of relief must have gone up from the lycée and the town hall.

NOTES

1. These photographs are reproduced in JC.
2. SL p. 13.
3. JC p. 17.
4. André Maurois, *Memoirs*.
5. JC p. 28.
6. JC p. 36.
7. SL pp. 1–2.
8. ARG.
9. JC mentions others in unpublished notes.
10. ARG p. 219.
11. JC pp. 63–4.
12. JC pp. 67–8.

13. See David Caute, *Communism and the French Intellectuals 1914–60*, André Deutsch 1964. For some interesting personal reminiscences, see A. Koestler, *The Invisible Writing*, A. Gide, *Journal*, A. Malraux, *Antimemoirs*.

3 Controversialist and Factory Hand

In the summer of 1932, before taking up a new teaching post at Auxerre, Simone Weil visited Germany. She stayed with a communist worker and his family in Berlin. The result of this visit was a series of articles in *La Revolution Prolétarienne* and *L'Ecole Emancipée* in which Simone analysed German politics in the year before Hitler came into power.[1] These articles are remarkable for their lucid exposition of the complex struggle in Germany; but more than that, they show an almost prophetic discernment of the political realities of that struggle. Simone quickly realized that the German communist party (the KPD), though in theory it was the strongest in Europe, was almost wholly lacking in revolutionary purpose and ability. The great majority of its members, Simone pointed out, were unemployed, and more than half of them had belonged to the party for less than a year. They were unorganized and untrained, and, like the rest of the six million unemployed in Germany, they had become weakened by near starvation. The revolutionary capability of the KPD was just about nil. Simone said that the calling of a strike of transport workers in Berlin in July, which gained the KPD 138,596 votes in the Reichstag election of that month, was merely a cloak to hide the party's bankrupt and incoherent policy. There was little doubt in her mind that the future lay with Hitler and the national socialists, in spite of a momentary setback due to a switch of some middle-class votes. The prospect horrified her. Even in 1932 Simone had no illusions about the Nazis. 'Hitler', she wrote, 'signifies organized massacre, the suppression of all liberty and of all culture.'

Simone Weil was especially bitter about the total failure of the Communist International to support the cause of the German workers against the growing power of the Nazis. The KPD was being used merely as a tool of Stalinist bureaucracy. 'It is clear', she wrote, 'that the interests of the bureaucracy of the Russian State do not coincide with the interests of the German workers. Their vital interest is to arrest fascist or military reaction; for the Russian State, it is simply to prevent Germany, whatever her internal regime may be, from turning against Russia by forming a bloc with France.'[2] Having devoted most of its energies to attacking the social democrats, the KPD was not only failing to oppose the Nazis, but, under orders from Moscow, was even supporting them. It was clear to Simone Weil that Russian communism held out no hope for a real transfer of power to the proletariat, and the party line in Germany confirmed her growing conviction that the Comintern bosses were interested only in the external security of the Soviet Union.[3] Later, she prophesied a non-aggression pact between Russia and Germany. It seemed to her that the totalitarian ambitions of Communist Russia and Nazi Germany were so alike as to be indistinguishable from each other. Events were to vindicate her judgment. By supporting Hitler (or at least by failing to oppose him), the KPD virtually signed its own death-warrant. On his attainment to power after the Reichstag fire in 1933, Hitler discarded his former allies. Blamed for the fire, the KPD was banned and its deputies imprisoned. Unbelievably, Russia closed her frontiers to the German communist refugees. Simone Weil pointed out how remarkable it was

35

that the 'capitalist' and 'Jewish' societies of the West should admit these refugees while their 'comrades' in the communist homeland cynically abandoned them to their fate in Hitler's concentration camps. She knew that the communist god had failed. The KPD had been utterly betrayed by the Communist International, and the political left in Germany, both socialist and communist, had been reduced to nonentity.

It had become clear to Simone Weil that State ownership of the means of production offered no guarantee that the proletariat would share in the control of industry. Hitler himself claimed to be a 'socialist' and had promised that the Nazi party would demolish the structure of capitalist power. In reality, however, the Nazis were more interested in the mystique of Nationalism than in social democracy. Simone Weil saw that a bureaucratic dictatorship, whether of the right or the left, meant control by party bosses whose real concern for the workers was absolutely nil. The only possibility was to withdraw from the struggle for political power at the top, and instead to promote confrontation between workers and employers within industry itself. It was in this area of action that Simone Weil felt herself to be most fully at home. She had already joined the syndicalist group associated with *La Révolution Prolétarienne* during her time in Le Puy. After her return from Germany she continued her syndicalist allegiance, though she was often a strange bedfellow. Her forthright condemnation of Russia's betrayal of the KPD earned the disfavour of those who still looked to Moscow for political inspiration, and she was also critical of the 'bureaucratic' tendency within syndicalism itself. She must sometimes have given the impression of being an enemy of the movement rather than a supporter of it. The truth was that her thought had shifted to a different level from that of the majority of her colleagues. She had identified another form of 'oppression' within industry itself – the oppression of 'functionalism'.

Her views were set out in an impressive article entitled 'Allons-nous vers la révolution prolétarienne?'[4] In the past, she wrote, humanity had known two principal forms of oppression: the slavery or servitude exercised by armed force, and the slavery or servitude exercised by wealth.[5] But there was also a third form of oppression which was not located in the time-honoured distinction between capital and labour, and which exposed a basic fallacy in Marxist theory. Marx had exalted the demand for ever-increasing production, and had believed that the degrading opposition between intellectual and manual work could be abolished. But, said Simone Weil, in the event the very opposite had happened. Greater productivity meant greater rationaliza-tion of industrial processes and therefore the division of labour into smaller and smaller functions or specialisms. In a highly developed modern industry, it was impossible for anyone to familiarize himself with all stages of the production process. No one could see further than his own function, and every worker was brought to the point of performing his function without knowing the overall plan into which his work would fit. The worker was dominated and limited by the machine which he operated. In the era of technocracy, the division of labour inevitably increased. 'To the opposition created by money between buyers and sellers of labour is added another opposition, created by the means of production itself, between those who dispose of the machine and those of whom the machine disposes ... the first of these oppositions can be abolished without bring-ing about the disappearance of the second.'[6] Simone therefore demanded that manual work be given its 'rightful dignity'. The worker should be given opportunity to acquire full knowledge of technique instead of receiving only

37

elementary training as a machine-minder. Intelligence should be given its 'proper object' so that manual work might no longer result in opaqueness of mind and spirit. The essential thing was to uphold, not the collective, but the individual as the supreme value.[7] 'Bureaucracy', said Simone Weil, 'always betrays.'

Simone's article drew a reply from no less a person than Trotsky. He said that Simone Weil had found consolation in a new cause – the defence of her personality against society. This, Trotsky said, was nothing but 'petit-bourgeois prejudice'.[8] From the standpoint of the political left, of course, Trotsky was quite correct, and his words indicate the uneasiness of Simone Weil's association with the revolutionary movement. Her feeling of repugnance towards collectivism and bureaucracy in all their forms made her more of an anarchist than a revolutionary.[9] As a strikingly independent thinker she was incapable of toeing any party line, even that proposed by people with whom she was basically in sympathy, and this meant that she always as it were had one foot in the political wilderness. Perhaps her attitude is best summed up in her own dictum: 'We must always be prepared to change sides like Justice – that fugitive from the winning camp.'[10]

As a political thinker and counsellor, Simone Weil was original and sometimes profound. As a political activist, however, she was more or less grotesque. By nature reserved and introspective, her attempts to achieve comradeship with trade-unionists often caused embarrassment, and demonstrations seem to have aroused in her an excitement which sometimes made her act foolishly. Jacques Cabaud tells us of one occasion when there was a general strike in Saint-Etienne. The miners swarmed into the streets and were charged by national guards on horseback. Simone was not there because her friends among the miners had kept their plans secret from her. They knew that her imprudence and her inability to run would have been bound to lead to her arrest. Cabaud adds that the miners themselves would probably have been arrested or beaten up while trying to protect her.[11] It would seem that Simone's activism was more often a liability than an asset to the trade-union cause. Her sympathies were genuinely and deeply felt, but her excitement and extremism made her presence on the streets both a worry and a danger to her friends.

Simone herself realized that she was in some measure open to a charge of dilettantism, of merely 'playing politics' without any genuine involvement in the life of those whose cause she supported. Being a person of unflinching honesty, she found this position intolerable. She had already worked on the land, but now she formed a plan for being employed in a factory as an unskilled labourer and living anonymously in a working-class district. During the period 1932-4, she had continued her work as a professional teacher, combining this with her political writing and activity as she had done at Le Puy. Her first school after her return from Germany in 1932 was the girls' lycée at Auxerre, which she had chosen because it was near Paris. She left the school after a year and took up a post at the lycée in Roanne, a manufacturing city sixty-five miles west of Lyons. Again she left after a year. As M.-M. Davy remarks, these changes from one school to another after only a year at each were not promotions but 'mutations'.[12] Wherever she went, Simone caused confusion. If it is true that only France could have produced a Simone Weil, it may also be true that only the French could have tolerated one! Her attitude towards her colleagues and superiors was eccentric to the point of rudeness, and her political notoriety could hardly fail to bring doubt and discredit upon the schools where she worked. One of her colleagues has said that Simone Weil lived with the school staff like a stranger, and recalls meal-times when she read Karl Marx, raising her eyes occasionally and looking at her fellow teachers as though she did not see them.[13] Much could be forgiven her for her brilliance of mind and her stimulating effect upon her pupils; but in the crucial test of examinations her girls did not do well and their parents were not pleased. Simone was experimenting with the technique of approaching philosophical problems through plays and novels, thereby anticipating the method later adopted by existentialist writers like Sartre and Marcel, and one cannot doubt that her classes must have been highly interesting to reasonably imaginative pupils. But perhaps Simone's teaching was not very helpful in pre-paring them for successful careers in a bourgeois society whose values she hated.

In June 1934, Simone applied to the Ministry of Education for a year's leave of absence 'for personal studies'. Officially, she was supposed to be preparing 'a philosophical treatise' on the relations between modern technology, social organi-zation, and culture, but in fact her intention was to realize her long-cherished ambition of becoming a factory worker. No doubt this could be regarded as 'field-work', though it was far from being merely a way of collecting material for her thesis. Simone was determined to plunge herself into working-class life and to let the iron of it really enter her soul. Her thesis was only a minor consideration and in fact she never completed it for publication. Even so, however, it is one of her best pieces of writing, combining hard-won experience with her usual lucid intelligence. Its title is 'Oppression and Liberty'.

On 4 December 1934, Simone Weil started work as a factory hand at the Alsthom electrical works in Paris. From the first day, she kept a diary in which she recorded her jobs and her impressions. What soon became evident to her was her sheer physical inability to do an adequate day's work. She was not dexterous by nature, she was plagued by headaches, and her strength was drained away by the incessant noise and dirt of the factory. At first, she was able to think of herself in heroic terms as a graduate teacher who had willed herself into a harsh and unusual situation; but as her exhaustion increased this consolation was no longer effective and she became deeply depressed by her servitude to the mechanism of her job and her inability to work and think at the same time. She realized why it was that factory workers were such poor revolutionaries.[14] The nature of their jobs and the tyranny of 'output' left them neither time nor energy for thought. Simone discovered that they did not even understand their own machines and were quite ignorant of the process of manufacture as a whole. What she had previously written in a more or less theoretical way about the oppression of 'function' was now being proved to her by direct experience. It reinforced some of her most important ideas.

After four months at the Alsthom works, Simone was laid off. She found another job with the firm of Carnaud, but even when she worked to the limit of her strength and speed she could achieve only half the expected rate. She lasted a month, being dismissed on 7 May. Finally, after tramping the streets for a number of weeks looking for work, she was employed by one of the most neurotic of all industries, that of motor-car manufacture. She began at the Renault works on 6 June, working from 2.30 to 10 p.m. As a completely unskilled worker, she was given humble and monotonous jobs like operating a drilling machine. She was got at by foremen who demanded higher output from her. In her diary she referred to one mechanic as a 'petit salaud' because he told her at the end of a hard day that she had done less than the required rate.[15] She felt that she herself was becoming a machine, unable to see an inch beyond her own job, always threatened with dismissal if she did not work faster, until, as she said some years later, she became so accustomed to brutality that she felt surprised when anyone spoke kindly to her. She also said that during her year in factories she had lost her youth and had received the brand of slavery upon her soul.[16]

It is, of course, easy to say that Simone Weil was totally unfitted for factory work and that her reactions to it were therefore abnormally dramatic. The ordinary worker, accustomed to using his hands, develops a skill which makes his actions mechanical and so minimizes the need for concentrated effort. Simone, however, would have replied that that was precisely her point. Physical action which is entirely separated from thought is a form of slavery because it turns a man into an object and denies his true nature as one whose actions are the product of his thinking. This, in fact, is one of the main arguments in Simone's essay on oppression and liberty.[17] Marx, she says, believed that improved production methods and the discovery of new forms of energy would reduce manual labour to a minimum so that everyone would have enough wealth and leisure to satisfy their desires. Simone, however, argues that this view is factually dubious and psychologically unsound. There are limits beyond which production methods cannot be further improved, and even if new forms of energy are discovered, they will still require human labour to win and refine and apply them. More important, however, is the objection that the Marxist utopia is based upon a mistaken estimate of the nature of human freedom. What is required is not a lifting of the ancient curse of manual work, but the transformation of manual work itself into 'the supreme value'. True freedom is not defined by the relationship between desires and their satisfaction, but by the relationship between thought and action. In the conditions of modern industry, manual work has been degraded because it has ceased to be related to thought. Simone's point is that such work is performed, not as the most satisfying expression of man's creative freedom to collaborate with the natural order, but merely as a way of earning money. Even agricultural work, she adds, has been reduced to the cash-nexus. The farm labourers thinks only of becoming rich enough to leave the land. The result is that work, so far from being a cause of joy and an expression of free consent, has become instead a mindless servitude.

Simone Weil saw that these conditions would not be changed by the kind of social and political revolution envisaged by Marxists. The transfer of industrial ownership to other hands would simply set up a new bureaucracy essentially similar to the old. It would make no difference whatever to the internal organization of industry itself.[18] What was needed was a kind of evolution in each industry from the present oppressive hierarchical system to a fraternity distinguished by mutual co-operation and esteem. In such a fraternity, there would no longer be a mechanical, unthinking submission to the demands of machines and the orders of superiors. All workers, manual, technical, and managerial alike, would see their own individual work as a contribution to an understood whole for which all were equally responsible. The difference between slavery and freedom, said Simone Weil, is the difference between reacting blindly to necessity and adapting oneself to the inner representation of necessity found in one's own mind. No amount of fraternal association would be able to eliminate from industry the necessities of the production process. Machines must still be operated, output must still be maintained. But the man who could *understand* necessity (in this case the whole interlocking organization of production), and whose work was self-directed by that understanding – such a man would no longer be necessity's slave but its master.

This possibility of free consent to necessity is a theme to which Simone Weil often reverts, and it plays an important part in her later religious and philosophical writing. In some respects, it corresponds to the Stoic 'love of fate' (*amor fati*), but in Simone's thought it is not simply a fatalistic submission to things as they are. In the social and political context, it means a repudiation of utopian dreams which merely divert attention from harsh realities and are powerless to change them. The great delusion is to think that machines will make men free. All the evidence points the other way. Machines enslave men to mechanical, degrading routine – not only in terms of their actual operation, but also in terms of the division of labour and the heartless, bureaucratic system of control which they generate. It is therefore quite useless to dream of a time when, by an automatic process of development, manual labour will no longer be required. The only way of improving anything is to start by identifying and accepting the necessities by which it is constituted. Then, and only then, can one begin to introduce some 'play in the cog-wheels' – that is, to make necessity itself a bearer of human values.

Simone ended her nine months' factory work in a state of complete exhaustion. What had affected her most, however, was not fatigue but humiliation. The real struggle had been a spiritual one – the need each day to try to snatch a little human dignity out of a cold, inhuman system.[19] It had made her more sensitive, not only to the affliction of the world, but perhaps also to the presence in humble people of a power to express that affliction and, in expressing, to transcend it. This may explain her intense response to an event which occurred soon after she gave up factory work. Her parents had taken her to Portugal for a holiday, and one evening she wandered off by herself and came to a small fishing village.

> I entered the little Portugese village, which alas was very wretched too, on the very day of its patronal festival. I was alone. It was the evening and there was a full moon. It was by the sea. The wives of the fishermen were going in procession to make a tour of the ships, carrying candles and singing what must certainly have been very ancient hymns of a heart-rending sadness. Nothing can give any idea of it. I have never heard anything so poignant unless it were the song of the boatmen on the Volga. There the conviction was suddenly borne in upon me that Christianity is pre-eminently the religion of slaves, that slaves cannot help belonging to it, and I among others.[20]

It may not be too much to say that in this experience lay the germ of Simone Weil's religious development.

NOTES

1. These articles are included in EHP.
2. EHP p. 138.
3. Compare A. Koestler's novel *Darkness at Noon* and John Strachey's comment on it in *A Strangled Cry*, Bodley Head 1962. Also A. Koestler and others, *The God that Failed* (ed. Crossman).
4. OL pp. 11–38. A. Camus refers to this article in *The Rebel*, Hamish Hamilton 1953, p. 185.
5. OL p. 21.
6. OL p. 22.
7. OL pp. 32–3.
8. JC p. 87.
9. Anarchism of an intellectual, non-violent type had something of a vogue in the 1930s. In England, there was a group who called themselves 'Philosophical Anarchists' whose aim was to preserve creative individual freedom against the levelling tendency of herd-values and State control. 'Mr Propter' in A. Huxley's novel *After Many a Summer* is an idealized portrait of such an anarchist. The French and Spanish anarchists were much more socially and politically committed and active.
10. GG p. 151.
11. JC p. 102–3.

12. MMD p. 17.
13. MMD p. 16.
14. SL p. 37.
15. CO p. 88.
16. WG p. 33.
17. OL: full title, *Réflexions sur les Causes de la Liberté et de l'Oppression sociale*.
18. SL p. 40.
19. SL pp. 30, 38.
20. WG pp. 33–4.

4   Reformer and Idealist

In the year 1935–6, we find Simone Weil trying to introduce
a little play into the cog-wheels of industry at managerial
level. She had applied for a new teaching post and had been
appointed to the girls' lycée at Bourges where one of her
pupils was a daughter of the director of the Foundries of
Rosières. The firm had built a new plant near Bourges with
houses for the workers set round it, and the management
made themselves responsible for the social welfare of their
employees. The system was thought to be an exceptionally
enlightened one at the time, and was comparable to the
well-known English example of Lever Brothers at Port
Sunlight. Its great weakness in Simone's eyes was that it
not only failed to give the workers any participation at the
organizational level, but even created states of mind in
which initiative and responsibility were stifled.

The chief engineer of the Rosières plant, however, was
trying in a tentative way to encourage ideas on the shop
floor, and he had introduced a question-box and a house
magazine into the factory. His name was Bernard, and
Simone Weil saw in him the possibility of putting some of
her own ideas into practice. She wrote an article for the
magazine in which she asked the workers to express their
views about conditions of employment in the factory with a
view to discussion with the management. Although she
framed this request with unusual tact, Bernard refused to
publish it on the ground that it had revolutionary under-

tones. Simone wrote him a disappointed letter. She pointed out that the essential thing was to give the workers dignity in their own eyes. The humiliating and servile conditions of their daily work and the contrast between their way of life and that of their employers inevitably produced class feeling, and it would be better to allow this feeling expression rather than let it smoulder beneath the surface.[1]

An article by Simone Weil which Bernard *did* publish was very different from her earlier proposal. It was an outline of the story of Sophocles' drama *Antigone*.[2] This may surprise us – until we remember that one of Simone Weil's passions was to introduce workers to the heritage of European culture. She believed that they would respond more readily to the literature of ancient Greece than those whose sensitivity had been blunted by bourgeois values, and she expressed to Bernard the ironical hope that he would not find *Antigone* subversive. The central theme of *Antigone* – the conflict between reasons of State and personal ideals – was very close to Simone's heart, and no doubt she would have found no difficulty in transferring it to the conditions of life at the Rosières foundry had she been given opportunity for discussion of her article with the workers.

Simone's correspondence with Bernard continued for several months. She suggested that she might be employed in the factory so that she could discover what the workers really thought and report their ideas to the management. It says much for Bernard's liberalism that he was evidently prepared to entertain this plan seriously, though he probably did not realize what a risk he would have been running. In the event, Simone came to feel that it would be wrong for her to take a job when so many local women were unemployed.

She returned to this idea, however, in a discussion with

another industrialist, Auguste Detoeuf, who was a manager of electrical companies in Paris and had in fact arranged for Simone's employment at the Alsthom works. Detoeuf seems to have been a man of exceptional idealism and humanity, and he sympathized with Simone's aims. Their correspondence coincided with a wave of stay-in strikes in France in the summer of 1936. Among other factories, the Renault works in Paris was occupied by the workers and Simone was delighted by this demonstration on the part of her former co-employees. She wrote to Detoeuf, however, saying that, when work was resumed, the men should be told that they must now accept some responsibility in factory organization. To this end, they should be encouraged to form technical, economic and social study groups in the factories so as to learn about the organization and management of an industrial concern. It was wrong, Simone thought, that the working class should gain concessions from the employers by 'crude force' without any sharing of responsibility.[3] No doubt Simone herself would have been more than ready to play a part in this education of the workers had not another crisis intervened which commanded her immediate attention – the Spanish civil war.

Even now, after thirty-four years, one can still recall the passionate feeling evoked by the drama in Spain. The French and British governments, after a period of indecision, settled for a policy of non-intervention, but to many western intellectuals this burking of the issue was contemptible. They saw the civil war as the first direct confrontation between the forces of fascist militarism and those of revolutionary freedom, though the issues in Spain itself were in fact far less clear-cut than they supposed. The war became a focus of the conflict between the right-wing and the left-wing camps in Europe. Germany and Italy supported Franco and the nationalists; Russia supported the republicans (though far less effectively). It was a war of unexampled brutality on both sides. For the first time in Europe (Mussolini had already used the technique in Abyssinia), towns and cities were subjected to saturation bombing. Prisoners were shot and civilians murdered. In a war in which the enemy was often hard to identify, treachery became a commonplace and vengeance a sacred duty.

A number of French and British intellectuals volunteered for the republican side. Among the British contingent were George Orwell, John Cornford, and Tom Wintringham. Ernest Hemingway arrived from America. France supplied, among many others, André Malraux (who became commander of the republican air force), Arthur Koestler (rather oddly representing the English *News Chronicle*) – and Simone Weil.

In Sartre's novel *The Age of Reason* (the title is ironical), there is a scene in which Mathieu, the professor of philosophy, encounters a sturdy beggar, an ex-soldier, in the street. The beggar tells him that he wants to get to Spain to fight in the civil war. Mathieu's immediate reaction is one of envy. He wishes that he too had the courage to dedicate himself to a definitive ideal. In this portrayal of his hero's feelings, Sartre represented the pull which the Spanish war exerted over many liberal intellectuals at the time. It seemed that here at last was the chance to by-pass the craven policy of co-existence and to take direct action against fascist aggression. Not surprisingly, in spite of her pacifism, Simone Weil was one of those to whom the pull was irresistible. Under cover as a journalist, she left Paris early in August 1936 for Barcelona to join the republican cause. Fortunately for her, her career in Spain was brief and inglorious.

Simone recorded her activities and impressions in her Spanish diary and in a letter which she subsequently wrote to Georges Bernanos, a well-known Catholic writer who had published a book entitled *Les Grands Cimetières sous la Lune* describing nationalist atrocities in Majorca. Simone was attached to a column of the anarchist forces under the command of a famous leader named Durruti, and she took part in a crossing of the river Ebro. The operation met no resistance, but an enemy plane dropped a small bomb. Simone 'felt no emotion at all'. She was much more afraid of being captured and shot. It was common knowledge that neither side took prisoners, and she heard stories of atrocities committed by her own side. She felt that she could have no moral objection to being shot, since she was herself compromised by such actions.

Richard Rees remarks that it was fortunate for Simone that she was in Spain during the early months of the war when, among the anarchists, a certain amount of tolerance still prevailed.[4] Later on, when attitudes had hardened, her critical forthrightness would have been suicidal. Certainly, she was no soldier. Her idealism, her imprudence, her inability to suspend her own judgment when she was under orders, and her sheer clumsiness with a rifle (according to Jacques Cabaud, she was a danger to friend as well as foe), all made her a liability and could have made her a menace. She was released by a happy accident. While cooking, she spilt some hot fat over her leg and was badly burnt. She was sent to a base hospital at Sitges near Barcelona where her parents collected her and took her back to Paris. She had been in Spain for two months.

Simone shared in the disillusion of most of the idealists who had volunteered to fight in Spain.[5] 'One sets out as a volunteer', she wrote, 'with the idea of sacrifice, and finds oneself in a war which resembles a war of mercenaries, only with much more cruelty and with less human respect for the enemy.'[6] What disgusted her most was the fact that the wretched Spanish peasants in whose cause the anarchists were supposed to be fighting were treated with off-hand condescension by the militia. The purpose of the struggle had been lost in a 'blood-polluted atmosphere' in which murder itself had become something of which to boast.

When she returned from Spain, Simone was physically at a low ebb. Her headaches became worse, she was dead tired, and her burnt leg was slow to heal. Her father applied to the Ministry of Education for sick-leave for her, and in the spring of 1937 she went off for a holiday in Switzerland and Italy. This period of respite included experiences which were of importance for the subsequent development of her interior life, and we shall return to it later.

In France itself, the occupation of factories by the workers in May–June 1936 had coincided with a general election in which the newly formed Popular Front, an alliance of socialists and communists, gained a sweeping majority of 380 in the Chamber of Deputies. The socialist leader, Léon Blum, became Prime Minister, but the communists refused to join his government and were thus able to claim credit for supporting the Popular Front without sharing its responsibilities. No doubt the PCF was, as usual, acting on orders from Moscow, though some of its members had taken warning from the disastrous effect of this policy in Germany and had opted out. The political alliance which created the Popular Front also involved an alliance among the trade-unions and a merging of the two rival organizations, the socialist CGT and the communist CGTU. Supporters of the trade-union cause, however, soon discovered that the merger had not eliminated the rivalry between the two camps. Many of them, including Simone Weil, were horrified by communist attempts to whitewash the Moscow trials, and Simone expressed the fear that 'a CGT subjected to the communist party would be a mere appendage to the Russian State'.[7] In a number of articles Simone returned to her old theme of the need to work out in industry itself the participation of workers in the organization of the production process. Richard Rees detects a rather 'scolding' tone in some of these articles.[8] Perhaps Simone was beginning to feel that her cause could make no headway so long as the unions were expending their energies on internal struggles for power.

The question of power, particularly as it affects relationships between nations, is the theme of one of Simone Weil's most distinguished essays, published in *Nouveaux Cahiers* on 1 and 15 April 1937 under the title, 'Ne recommençons pas la guerre de Troie'.[9] Her main point is that the majority of human conflicts, like the war between Greece and Troy, are 'conflicts with no definable objective'. The Greeks and Trojans massacred each other for ten years on account of Helen, for whom none of them (except Paris) cared two straws. In the conflicts of today, Helen's place has been taken by abstract entities (or rather, non-entities) spelled with capital letters, which are even more devoid of significance than Helen herself. Precisely because these conflicts are literally conflicts about nothing, they are by far the most dangerous. Genuine differences of interest are resolvable by reasoned compromise, but when the difference is merely between one senseless absolute and another, compromise is impossible and war continues by a kind of self-perpetuation with each side trying to justify the blood it has already spilt. Simone gives several examples of this 'murderous absurdity', one of which is the opposition between fascism and communism. One has only to examine the present-day meaning of the two words, she says, to discover two almost identical political and social conceptions. Therefore the opposition between them is strictly meaningless. If a war between fascists and communists were to take place (she means in France, where an extreme right-wing party called 'Croix de Feu' had recently become prominent), 'it would make the Trojan war look perfectly reasonable by comparison. . . . A phantom Helen is a substantial reality compared to the distinction between fascism and communism.'

What has been forgotten or ignored, Simone continues, is the fact that there are no social or political absolutes anywhere. This is true even in the case of the real distinction between dictatorship and democracy. In every social organism there is a compound of both in different proportions. Similarly, it is nonsensical to put the blame for social ills on 'capitalism', a word which converts the complex realities of economic relationships into a meaningless abstraction and effectively prevents the posing of questions about the laws and conventions which control economic life. 'All the absurdities which make history look like a prolonged delirium have their root in one essential absurdity, which is the nature of power.' Absurdities can be made to appear reasonable when they become rallying cries for power and prestige. Thus 'the national interest' is really defined by the power of the State to make war, because 'between one prestige and another there can be no equilibrium'. This is the impasse from which humanity can only escape by some miracle.

As Simone was soon to know, there was no miracle and humanity did not escape. The ambitions of Hitler were far greater than either she or anyone else supposed when her article was written, and she came to regret her uncompromising pacifism. It is true that the war produced numberless buffooneries, but it is not true that it was essentially a war about 'vacuous entities or abstractions'.

The distinction between democracy and dictatorship became more decisive than Simone had allowed, though she was right in thinking that, in conditions of war, the democratic nations would themselves be forced to adopt a large amount of dictatorial control. Her essay retains its value as a warning against allowing bogus absolutes like Freedom, Democracy, Nation, Order, Security, Revolution, Capitalism (Clive Bell called them 'expensive vocables')[10] to become substitutes for thought and analysis. The passing of time has not reduced their number or their influence.

In October 1937, Simone began to teach again, this time at the lycée of Saint-Quentin, her fifth school in seven years. But her headaches became exceptionally severe and she had to resign at the end of her first term. She spent the year 1938 at home with her parents. It was evidently a year of crisis for her and it marks the transition to the second and more mysterious stage of her development. She was less active politically, though she continued to write articles. The year 1938 was, of course, the period in which events began to gather the momentum which culminated in the Second World War. In March, Hitler invaded Austria and entered Vienna on the thirteenth. This 'Anschluss' opened the way to Czechoslovakia, whose Sudeten Germans had already been held up to pity by German propaganda. Chamberlain attempted negotiation with Hitler, but the outcome was the Munich agreement of 29 September which provided for German occupation of the Sudetenland by 10 October. These terms were accepted by the Czech government on 30 September.

Chamberlain and the French Prime Minister Daladier (who had replaced Léon Blum after the failure of the Popular Front government in the summer of 1938) have been regarded as the upholders of a shameful policy of appeasement which made war inevitable. With hindsight, we can see that their fundamental mistake was to think that Hitler was open to reasonable persuasion. But we forget that their policy represented the feelings of the great majority of ordinary British and French citizens. No one wanted to go to war for the sake of what seemed to be a remote and unimportant country, and it was easy to be persuaded that the Sudeten Germans were an oppressed minority whose desire for liberation was not unreasonable. Like many others, Simone Weil supported Franco-British policy and maintained the pacifist position, though we find her saying in an article published on 25 May that Hitler would probably be turned back only by force of arms. Her pacifism, like that of others, finally collapsed when German troops entered Prague on 15 March 1939. She explained her change of view by saying that pacifism is right so long as it works; when it ceases to work, one cannot continue to be a pacifist without moral treachery.

The years 1931–9 had been, for Simone Weil, years of intense activity. With her professional duties as a teacher, she had combined a deep involvement in trade-unionism and had written articles, essays, and innumerable letters on social and political questions. In addition, she had worked as a labourer in factories and on the land, and had fought (though only for a short time) in Spain. All this, we must remember, had been done by someone who was never really well and who was plagued by terrible headaches. What had distinguished her from most left-wing idealists had been the depth of her compassion for the oppressed, and her utter refusal to sacrifice individual and personal values to political doctrine and bureaucratic power. Her total identification with the workers and the hardships she willingly shared with them may have blinded her to the genuine problems of managements trying to grapple with declining markets and a chronic shortage of capital; her ideas often seemed extremist and impracticable even to such enlightened men as Bernard and Detoeuf.[11] But there was no doubting her sincerity or her commitment. She went her own way and she thought her own thoughts irrespective of all political camps and party interests. One of her most conspicuous and no doubt most irritating qualities was her intransigent honesty, and perhaps in the end we must conclude that her dislike of pragmatism made her a bad practitioner of the art of the possible. Perhaps her true vocation was to put the practitioners in mind of those ideals which, because they are impossible in a fallen world, are too often and too easily forgotten.

NOTES

1. SL pp. 40–2.
2. SG pp. 57–62.
3. SL pp. 59–60.
4. RR pp. 34–5.
5. E.g. A. Koestler, *Spanish Testament*, London 1937; G. Orwell, *Homage to Catalonia*, Penguin 1968, and 'Looking back on the Spanish War', reprinted in a collection of Orwell's essays entitled *England My England*, London 1953. The fullest history of the Spanish war in English is Hugh Thomas, *The Spanish Civil War*, Eyre & Spottiswoode 1961.
6. SL p. 108.
7. JC p. 153.
8. RR p. 41.
9. ET 'The Power of Words' in SE pp. 154–71.
10. In *Civilisation*.
11. See her letter to Detoeuf and his reply in SL pp. 61–9.

5   Spiritual Autobiography

In a letter to Father Perrin written on 15 May 1942, Simone Weil gave an account of what she called her 'spiritual autobiography'.[1] She described how, in adolescence, she had come to the conclusion that 'when one hungers for bread one does not receive stones'. At that time, she says, she had not read the gospel, but from earliest childhood she had always had the Christian idea of love for one's neighbour, to which, like the Stoics, she had given the name of Justice. For the time being, this had sufficed. To have gone further and accepted Catholic dogma would have been an act of intellectual dishonesty.

Nevertheless, Simone continued, she had had three contacts with Catholicism which 'really counted'. One had been the experience in a Portuguese fishing village which had produced in her the conviction that Christianity was the religion of slaves and that she, as a slave, could not help belonging to it. The next 'contact' had been during her holiday in Italy in 1937 when she had spent 'two marvellous days' in Assisi. In the little chapel where St Francis used to pray, something compelled her for the first time in her life to go down on her knees.[2] Lastly, in 1938 when on holiday with her mother, she had spent Holy Week and Easter at Solesmes where she had followed all the liturgical services. In spite of splitting headaches, she had responded deeply to the beauty of the chanting and the words. 'The Passion of Christ', she said, 'entered into my being once and for all.'

At Solesmes, Simone had met a young English Catholic who introduced her to the English metaphysical poets of the seventeenth century. Later, she had learnt George Herbert's poem 'Love', and during one of her recitations of the poem, as she said, 'Christ himself came down and took possession of me'.

Simone had considered that the problem of 'God' was rationally insoluble, since, by definition, God is the supreme value and cannot be demonstrated. What she had not foreseen was that there could be real contact between a human being and God. At Solesmes, she had found love at the centre of pain – 'a presence more personal, more certain, and more real than that of any human being'.[3] The Passion of Christ had reached her in affliction. As she was to say later, the Cross mediates between the infinite goodness of God and the brutal necessity of the world. That was how, for Simone Weil, God himself had solved the problem of God.

There have been those who have doubted whether Simone Weil ever became a Christian in any definable sense. She told Fr Perrin that her religious experiences had led her on to a discovery of Christian values in non-Christian writings and traditions, especially the Iliad, Plato, the mystery religions of Greece and Egypt, and the Bhagavad-Gita of Hinduism. Moreover, she steadfastly refused to accept baptism, explaining to Fr Perrin that she did not wish to separate herself from the great mass of unbelievers and from the many things outside the church which she loved. Although Fr Perrin and Simone's other Catholic friend Gustave Thibon believed that she was profoundly Christian, some Catholic commentators have been much less certain. Charles Moeller, for example, though he greatly admired her life, thought that her religious ideas were Gnostic and detected in them what seemed to him to be an obsession with sex.[4] Other writers have seen Simone Weil as a disappointed revolutionary who found refuge in quietism, or as a purveyor of existential anguish like Sartre, or simply as an unbalanced nihilist. It is possible to lift material from Simone's writings which lends colour to all these charges. She certainly felt herself under no obligation to confine her speculations within the straitjacket of Christian orthodoxy. She had never shown much respect for orthodoxies of any kind. But it is the vast range of her ideas and vision that makes her so much a prophet of our time. She was a great crosser of boundaries, and the present movement of thought across religions, cultures and disciplines is no more than a tentative version of what had already occurred in the speculations of Simone Weil thirty years ago. For Simone, there was no subject which did not have religious implications, none which did not speak of values and ends as well as means. One of the most fascinating features of her religious and philosophical writing is the use she makes of analogies from mathematics and the sciences. She found deep religious insights in folk-lore. She read history as a conflict between the forces which degrade man and those which dignify him. She discovered Christian intuitions in the ancient literatures of Egypt, Greece, India and China. This synthesizing power of her mind, this ability to identify the great things which are always the same throughout history and the world, however much the details may differ – this is what gives to Simone Weil's thought its inexhaustible power to stimulate and provoke. To ask whether her ideas were 'orthodox' in the narrow sense in which that word is usually understood is like asking whether a giant is a dwarf.

In one vital respect, however, Simone Weil was perhaps more Christian than many who call themselves by that name. The centre of her experience and her thought was occupied by the Passion of Christ. We have seen that it was during the liturgy of Holy Week at Solesmes, when her headaches were at their most intense, that Simone became aware of the divine love present in affliction. The essay she later wrote on 'The Love of God and Affliction' is one of the most moving Good Friday meditations in Christian literature.[5] She understood, as few have really done, the horror of man's forsakenness in a brutal, inhuman world. She knew how easily the values created by one generation can be destroyed by the next, how constantly force imposes its will on weakness, how invariably Justice flees from the camp of the conquerors. The God who reached out to Simone Weil at Solesmes was the God of the cross, the God of the concentration camp, the God of slaves, the God of those in pain and despair, the God of the victims of poverty and contempt. For it is precisely when all the bogus protective structures have collapsed, when the soul is 'pulverized' or nihilated, when it cries out, as the soul of Jesus did, in its helplessness and pain – it is precisely then that God is discovered in the darkness and love shapes itself in the void. That is what Simone Weil understood and that is how she understood. And although the cross may not be the whole of Christianity, yet without it the rest is a dream.

When she described her religious experiences to Fr Perrin, Simone remarked that she had never then read any mystical works. This reference suggests that she interpreted her experiences in a mystical sense, and she later came to value the writings of St John of the Cross and Meister Eckhart. The volume of her private notes published under the title *La Connaissance surnaturelle* opens with an account of another experience which she did not mention to Fr Perrin. It was a mysterious encounter with one who seemed to lead her to an attic where he gave her bread and wine and lay down with her on the floor. Simone's description suggests a kind of waking dream which probably took place in 1941 or '42 when she was in Marseilles. It indicates the type of mystical contact with the divine in which intellectual activity is suspended and the soul loses its virginity. Clearly, a psychological explanation is possible, but it is unnecessary to offer such an explanation as an alternative to the mystical one. The divine reality comes to the soul at its point of openness and need. There is no reason to think that psychological need is unconnected with spiritual need or that it calls for totally different kinds of fulfilment. Mysticism uses the language of physical love because only such language can express the soul's experience of penetration by the divine. Simone herself puts forward the view that the mystical use of the language of love is the primary use, because love in its primal meaning is directed towards the beauty of the universe and physical love is a transference of that love to a particular 'object'.[6] Whether or not that is so, it seems superficial and inadequate to offer psychological explanations of the 'nothing but' kind.

Pure mysticism is the way of negation, the nihilation of knowledge and thought and attachment until the soul passes into the 'dark night' beyond which it is identified with the transcendent Being of God.

> I said to my soul, be still, and wait without hope
> For hope would be hope for the wrong thing; wait without love
> For love would be love of the wrong thing; there is yet faith
> But the faith and the love and the hope are all in the waiting.
> Wait without thought, for you are not ready for thought:
> So the darkness shall be the light, and the stillness the dancing.[7]

Eliot's well-known lines, which were in part inspired by the words of St John of the Cross, express the process of detachment from the self which is common to all mystical vision.

Simone Weil spoke of 'waiting on God' in that stillness

and patience of soul which she liked to refer to by the Greek word *hypomene*. There is every reason to believe that she experienced moments of intense spiritual awareness and that much of her religious writing was an attempt to articulate that awareness. 'Man escapes from the laws of this world', she wrote, 'but only for the space of a flash of lightning. Moments of pause, of contemplation, of pure intuition, of mental void, of acceptance of the moral void. It is through such moments that he is able to approach the supernatural.'[8]

Mysticism raises a number of difficult problems for Christian doctrine. First, all mystics tend to resemble each other across all religions, and the distinctiveness of the gospel revelation is lost. Second, in its detachment from the world, mysticism tends to regard history and knowledge as obstacles to the soul's intercourse with the divine reality. Third, it tends to discount human personality and relationships. Meister Eckhart, for example, thought that detachment was superior to love. Fourth, it tends to ignore the ethical commands of the gospel and to by-pass the duty of ameliorating the conditions of human life. Fifth, it is independent of the sacramental and corporate life of the church.[9]

How far was Simone Weil a 'pure' mystic? We have seen that she found Christian intuitions in other faiths and other cultures, and that she refused baptism into the Roman Catholic church. But did her awareness of God also carry with it a negation of her concern for the world? Did she retreat into quietism? Did she give up her intellectualism? Did she, in short, become a wholly different person from the political thinker and social activist of 1931–8?

The answer to these questions is certainly 'no', but before we attempt to explain why, an important point must be made. Simone Weil was a 'mystic' at least in the sense that the God of her experience and belief was beyond space and

63

time. She did not believe, as many of those who share her secular concern today believe, that God is found only in that concern. She was fond of quoting Plato's saying that an infinite distance separates the goodness of God from the necessity of the world, and much of her speculation was an attempt to understand how that infinite distance might be bridged. That it *could* be bridged she had no doubt, and we shall see later how she thought the bridges might be built. But for Simone Weil the word 'God' was never merely a pious name for man's own ideals and aspirations: the God in whom she believed was the God of holiness, the God of perfection, the God who is 'high and lifted up' beyond the world of multiplicity and change. Ultimately, man's experience of this God could be spoken of only in terms of paradox – his voice is silence, his presence is darkness – because he is beyond all human power of expression and he appears only when man reaches the limit of his thought and knowledge. In this understanding of the divine reality, Simone Weil was a mystic in the sense in which, for example, Plato and Dionysius the Areopagite were mystics.

Nevertheless, it is impossible to fit Simone Weil into any neatly defined category. She found much that was congenial to her in Plato, but she did not follow the tendency implicit in Platonism to fund all value into the supernatural and to abdicate from responsibility to the world. Simone's mysticism seems to have made her even more passionately concerned about the world and its human affliction. Any account of her life must try to explain why this should have been so.

We must go back to her time of social and political activism. What seems to emerge from her experience and writings during that period is the conviction that suffering and evil, though they have a social and organizational aspect, are basically spiritual problems. Marx had claimed

64

to eliminate fatality and tragedy from human life, to liberate man from necessity and determination by a re-ordering of political power and rationalization of social and economic organization. But Simone had discovered the paradox that elimination of necessity is a destruction of the freedom of the spirit. The necessity she had in mind is the spiritual necessity that action be the product of thought. In a bureaucratized system, a hierarchical order is set up which divides men into those who dispose of the machines and those of whom the machines dispose. In other words, thought and action become separated, until the manual worker is only part of a mindless, mechanical process, and the boss never dirties his hands. Essentially, this process removes necessity and replaces it by force, and it is by force that men are reduced to slavery.

The separation of thought from action also makes it impossible for man to recognize another 'necessity', and that is the order of the world itself. Thought is the means by which man represents to himself the laws which govern the world. In his recognition of the necessity of these laws, man is enabled to accord to them his free, intelligent consent. His work then becomes his dignity because it expresses his spiritual freedom. But when thought is suppressed, the laws of the world become a tyranny, and again necessity is replaced by force, the main cause of human suffering.

In her social and political writings up to 1938, Simone Weil expressed these ideas without any religious reference. But it is fairly obvious that they point in that direction, and for Simone it was not a very big step to link the necessity of the world with a divine Creator. That is what she did in her essay entitled 'Forms of the Implicit Love of God' which she probably wrote in April 1942.

God causes this universe to exist, but he consents not to command it, although he has the power to do so. Instead, he leaves two other forces to rule in his place. On the one hand there is the blind necessity attaching to matter, including the psychic matter of the soul, and on the other the autonomy essential to thinking persons.

By loving our neighbour we imitate the divine love which created us and all our fellows. By loving the order of the world we imitate the divine love which created this universe of which we are a part.[10]

Man's free consent to the necessity of the world requires a kind of self-renunciation comparable to the self-renunciation of God in his act of creation. This is one of the ways by which the soul becomes open to the divine love.

> To empty ourselves of our false divinity, to deny ourselves, to give up being the centre of the world in imagination, to discern that all points in the world are equally centres and that the true centre is outside the world, this is to consent to the rule of mechanical necessity in matter and of free choice at the centre of each soul. Such consent is love.[11]

To Simone Weil, the necessity or order of the world is also its beauty, and in her essay on the Timaeus of Plato she says that 'the word beauty speaks to every heart'. The beauty of the world is one of the forms of the implicit love of God, one of the 'bridges' between man and God. It is present in all the preoccupations of secular life, but it is mutilated, distorted and soiled. 'If it were made true and pure it would sweep all secular life in a body to the feet of God, it would make the total incarnation of the faith possible.'[12]

Richard Rees remarks that although Simone wrote a lot about beauty in general terms as 'the beauty of the world', she seldom descends to particulars.[13] That is true if we think of the beauty of the world in the romantic, Wordsworthian sense of 'meadows, lakes, and streams'. But as we have seen, that is not really what Simone meant. For her, the beauty of the world is its *order*, its obedience to 'necessity', its manifestation of form and limit. Man's apprehension of this beauty is essentially an intellectual apprehension, and it is realized above all in the unfolding of mathematical forms and scientific laws. Nature is 'obedient' to these forms and laws, and that is why she offers us a lesson in self-renunciation. As we contemplate this beauty, this order of the world, we are led into a similar state of self-renunciation. We no longer see ourselves as the centre of the world, we give up our 'false divinity', we renounce our ambition to 'command', we abandon the illusion that we can create our own reality. In short, we become detached from our 'personality', our selfish ego, and that is the meaning of love. The beauty of nature performs the same kind of office as that performed by human affliction. It opens the way to that negation of self beyond which lies the mystical vision. In Simone Weil's thought, detachment is not attained by the negative way of pure mysticism which denies all value to the world. It is precisely *in* the world and *through* the world that the soul becomes accessible to God. The beauty of the world and the affliction of men create in us an image of the divine self-emptying and identify us with the compassion of God for the work of his hands. We may say that Simone Weil's mysticism is essentially a mysticism of creation and the cross. We shall see later how she was able to use mathematical and scientific analogies in her exposition of it.

We have tried to show that Simone Weil's mysticism, so far from detaching her from the world, actually involved her more deeply in it. 'If Simone Weil has any claim to sanctity', writes E. W. F. Tomlin, 'it lies not in her conversion at a particular time, but in the steady convergence of her whole being upon a point which throughout life she kept clearly in view.'[14] It is possible to give Simone's mystical experiences an exaggerated importance, especially if we think they represent a 'connaissance surnaturelle' which most of us cannot share. Simone's mystical experiences did not exempt her from 'the intolerable wrestle with words and meanings'. And her conclusions stand in their own right without any need of backing by an appeal to the occult. She was not self-deceived. Her writing is always an effort to make the mystery of faith intelligible. She saw little value in language which impresses by its impenetrable obscurity, its deliberate torturing of meanings, its indulgence in absurd paradoxes. She remained a pupil of Alain in the sense that she did not allow emotional mystification to soften and blur her intellectual rigour. Even her hatreds are well-argued hatreds! What delighted her most was the discovery of a hidden relationship, an illuminating comparison, an unexpected resemblance which opened mystery to the understanding. She was, of course, far from being a cold, sceptical analyst of ideas. Her own involvement in what she writes is evident on every page. But her passion was above all an intellectual passion, and she believed that the vision of God came to those who were willing not only to 'wait' for God (*attente*) but also to 'attend' to God (*attention*). She once said that it was the greatest possible disaster to wrestle with God and not be beaten,[15] but it is clear that to her the most terrible thing was not to wrestle at all. Only if we wrestle can we be brought to the point at which we recognize our inability to win, and only then can we turn towards God in patience and 'attente', confident that his love will answer our humility.

NOTES

1. WG pp. 28–49.
2. SW described her Italian holiday in letters to her mother and to Jean Posternak, SL 79–87.
3. SL p. 140.
4. CM pp. 220–55.
5. WG pp. 76–94 and SNLG pp. 170–98.
6. WG p. 126.
7. T. S. Eliot, *Collected Poems 1909–62*, Faber & Faber 1963, p. 200.

8. GG p. 11.

9. See Meister Eckhart, *Selected Treatises and Sermons*, Collins Fontana 1963.

10. WG p. 114.

11. WG p. 115.

12. WG p. 118.

13. RR p. 85.

14. EWFT p. 59.

15. Quoted by RR p. 145.

6 Land Worker in the South of France

The period between the outbreak of war in September 1939 and the French armistice in the summer of 1940 was spent by Simone Weil in Paris. That she had not retreated into some kind of spiritual solitude (though she was reading the Bhagavad-Gita and learning Sanscrit) is evident from two essays which she wrote at this time. Although one of them was about the Iliad and the other mainly about the Roman Empire, they were both directed towards the immediate situation – so much so, in fact, that the French censor would allow only the second part of her essay on Rome to be published. The theme of the two pieces is 'force'. In the Iliad essay,[1] Simone holds up to admiration the recognition by the Greeks of the tragic sense of life. Tragedy is discovered in the fact that all men are, without exception, subjected to force. Men are not free. They are enslaved by oppression, by selfish passion, by herd-values, by self-deception. In the Iliad, Greeks and Trojans alike are under the sway of force, and the poet feels an equal compassion for both. There is no contempt for the victims of force because all men are equally its victims. It is this recognition which fills the poem with bitterness – the only justifiable bitterness, says Simone Weil, because it springs from a recognition of what is true and releases a universal compassion. Simone found a similar recognition in only a very few other works of western literature: some of the

Greek tragedies, the gospels, the *Phèdre* of Racine, and Shakespeare's *King Lear*.

Simone contrasts the universal humanity of the Iliad with the ruthless ambition of the Hebrews and Romans. Both these nations believed themselves to be exempt from the common human misery. The Hebrews thought that their God had chosen them and would exalt them over their enemies if they were obedient. The Romans believed that they were the nation chosen to be the mistress of the world. Both nations despised their fallen enemies and claimed to possess an indefeasible superiority over other peoples. In her long essay on totalitarianism entitled 'Some Reflections on the Origins of Hitlerism',[2] Simone showed that 'reasons of State' were, for the Romans, the complete justification for treachery, massacre, slavery, and abominable cruelties. The Romans were the first to develop the art of psychological warfare. They would alternate utter ruthlessness with fair promises and perfidious kindness. Their promises to invaded peoples were merely a base technique to undermine resistance, and their occasional acts of generosity were invariably prompted by self-interested motives. In a word, the Roman Empire was a totalitarian dictatorship which almost succeeded in obliterating the Greek spirit for ever.

Hitler and the Nazis, Simone continued, were the last in the line of descendents from Rome – a line which included the mediaeval Roman church, the Spain of Philip II, the France of Louis XIV and Richelieu, and Napoleon. In Hitler, Europe had found the most remarkable imitator of Rome who had yet appeared.

The claim is made that Napoleon propagated, with his sword, the French Revolutionary ideas of liberty and equality; but what he chiefly propagated was the idea of the centralized State, the State as the sole fount of authority and object of devotion. This conception of the State . . . has reached its *ne plus ultra* in Germany today.[3]

71

It is entirely characteristic of Simone Weil that she should include her own country among those which have imitated 'the great beast' of Rome. Not many people were clear-sighted or courageous enough in 1940 to question the assumed right of the western democracies to fight under the banners of Freedom and Justice. Simone's ideas about the nature of true patriotism will occupy us in a later chapter; for the moment it is perhaps sufficient to notice that her deep love of France did not include a suspension of her moral judgment. The French censor, however, had a different opinion about patriotism in time of war.

But Simone's patriotism cannot be questioned. The year 1940 saw another and very different product of her thought. This was a proposal that a squad of volunteer nurses should be formed to serve in the front line with the troops.[4] Simone read up enough medicine to learn that many lives could be saved by immediate first-aid, and she suggested that her front-line nurses, equipped with bandages, blood-plasma, etc. could do invaluable medical work. But more than that, she thought that the psychological effect of their presence would be considerable. The nurses would be recognized as a 'suicide corps' of devoted women whose indifference to their personal safety would more than match the brutal heroism of Hitler's young men. The courage of these women would 'demonstrate to the world that we are worth more than our enemies'. Needless to say, Simone herself would have been a member of the team.

Simone communicated her idea to a French senator, and it was 'favourably reported on' by the Army Commission of the Senate at the War Ministry in May 1940. However, as Simone said later in a letter to Maurice Schumann, 'owing to the rapid evolution of events, no attempt at putting it into practice was possible'.

Simone remained in Paris until shortly before the arrival

of the Germans and then departed to join her parents in Vichy. She was horrified by the armistice and did not hesitate to apply the word 'treason' to the behaviour of left-wing intellectuals who, like herself, had espoused the pacifist cause before the war and had undermined the will to resist fascist aggression. She decided that she must continue the struggle, and she determined to get to England to join de Gaulle and the Free French. It was intolerable to her that France should have given in, and she considered it a delusion to suppose that the values of civilization would, by some kind of mysterious self-preservation, survive the onslaught of 'the great beast'. Such preservation would be possible only if men could be found who valued beauty above power, who were willing to renounce 'the universal ambition of men to wield all the power they can' in favour of the fragile, painfully cultivated flowers of civilization which power destroys. That is the theme of Simone's play *Venice Preserved*, which she began to write when she was in Vichy.[5] The city of Venice is saved from destruction through the betrayal of one of the conspirators, a man named Jaffier, who in the end is unable to tolerate the prospect of burning, rape and pillage – the reduction of Venice and her people to a rootless, withered existence. The play has a wistful quality, as though the author were telling us that the triumph of beauty over power is so rare as to be almost a miracle. Certainly, Simone's reading of history led her to that conclusion. As we have seen, she considered that the Roman Empire had almost succeeded in extinguishing human values for ever, and she saw no reason for assuming the easy posture of those who merely sit back and wait for the downfall of the big battalions. She returned to this theme in her essays on the civilization of Languedoc, which we shall examine later.

In October 1940, Simone and her parents left Vichy for Marseilles with the intention of obtaining a passage to America, from which country Simone herself hoped to travel to England. Twenty months were to pass before they were successful.

It was during her time in Marseilles that Simone met a person who has already been mentioned in these pages – Father Perrin, who was then at the Dominican convent in the city. For Simone (and for us) it was a meeting of great good fortune. Fr Perrin seems to have been a man of exceptional wisdom, sympathy and patience. He was the first and only priest whom Simone really got to know, and he provided her with the 'audience' which her fermenting ideas needed. He himself claimed that he had done no more for her than any priest would have done, but he seems to have won her confidence when others might well have failed.[6] Simone expressed her profound gratitude to him in the letters she wrote, which he later published with an Introduction under the title *Attente de Dieu* in 1950. They reveal much of Simone's character – a deeply felt personal affection combined with the old intransigence and honesty which we have so often noticed in her. She was afraid that her gratitude to Fr Perrin and her fear of hurting the feelings of so good a friend might tempt her to abandon her convictions and principles. It is hardly necessary to say that she resisted the temptation successfully! He entirely failed to convince her that she ought to accept baptism into the church, and his patient efforts to remove some of her errors of judgment – over the Old Testament for example – found no response. 'I believe', he wrote, 'that her soul is incomparably superior to her genius and that, with her whole being, she is a witness of the living God.'[7]

The first good service which Fr Perrin performed for

Simone was to introduce her to his friend Gustave Thibon, a farmer and social philosopher who lived in the Ardèche. Simone wanted to work on the land (as a Jew she was forbidden to teach), so Fr Perrin asked Thibon to take her into his home and find her a job. Thibon has given us two vivid descriptions of his meeting with Simone. He confesses that he was at first reluctant to saddle himself with 'a militant supporter of the extreme left', but he changed his mind because, among other reasons, he was unwilling 'to spurn a soul which Destiny had placed in my path'.[8] At the moment of Simone's arrival, Thibon was called away, and he returned to find her sitting on a tree-stump, gaunt and dishevelled, contemplating the Rhône valley. 'Then', he writes, 'I saw her gaze relaxing slowly from contemplation to normal vision: the intensity and purity of that look were of such a kind that she seemed to be contemplating interior abysses along with the wonderful panorama that opened at her feet, and that the beauty of her soul took something from the moving majesty of the landscape.'[9]

As he had foreseen, Thibon did not find Simone an easy guest. She battered him with argument, she disturbed his household by her determination to eat as little and to be as uncomfortable as possible. After a time, she decided to live in an old, half-ruined farm situated on the banks of the Rhône because she found Thibon's house 'too comfortable'. Yet when Simone's reserve had been overcome, she showed what was best in her. 'She was just then beginning to open with all her soul to Christianity, a limpid mysticism emanated from her; in no other human being have I come across such familiarity with religious mysteries; never have I felt the word *supernatural* to be more charged with reality than when in contact with her.'[10] Those words of Thibon – a man who, like Fr Perrin, was not easily deceived – indicate the quality of *authenticity* in Simone Weil which is also unmistakably present in her writings. As E. W. F. Tomlin remarks, 'she was all of a piece, even if it was an odd piece'.[11] But her eccentricities were never the playing of a studied part. She literally hated the kind of comfort and sufficiency with which most of us are only too happy to insulate ourselves from the 'affliction' of the world. She once said that when she contemplated the sufferings of Christ, she committed the sin of envy. It is impossible to understand Simone Weil if we fail to recognize that that statement was for her the simple truth.

In his Preface to *The Need for Roots*, T. S. Eliot remarked that Simone Weil was a person 'in whom one detects no sense of humour'. It is true that most of her writing was on a plane where humour seems inappropriate, though she was capable of mordant observations on the follies of men which certainly have a humorous quality. Gustave Thibon, however, tells us that 'in intimacy she was a charming and lively companion; she knew how to joke without bad taste and could be ironical without unkindness'.[12] Nevertheless, one has the impression that few people ever saw this more 'human' side of her character. Her attempts in her earlier years to make friends among working men and women suggest a feeling of strain and artificiality – though we should not forget that she won the admiration and affection of many.[13] Above all, of course, one detects in the intransigence of her convictions a quality which sometimes irritated and repelled even those who were her friends. In her refusal to accept normal hospitality, she gave little thought to the inconvenience to others which this often entailed, and although she herself was an exceptionally generous 'giver', she was a very bad 'receiver'. She seems to have carried her independence of mind and body to absurd lengths, and on the ordinary human level she was a 'difficult' person – at least among members of her own social class.

Gustave Thibon admits that this was so, and he thinks that in some respects she was curiously immature. Perhaps, as he says, she had not yet learnt to live with her own genius, though *of* that genius there could be no doubt whatever.

Simone worked each day on the land 'with tireless energy', and often ate nothing but wild blackberries for a midday meal. As always, she tried to interest her peasant co-workers in the things of the mind, and Thibon remembers a young Lorraine girl who was subjected to a magnificent commentary on the Upanishads. 'The poor child nearly died with boredom, but shyness and good manners prevented her from saying anything.'14 Simone believed that the great classics of literature spoke more directly to working-class people than to those whose responses had been blunted by sophistication and material comfort, and she often made comical over-estimations of the capacity of peasants and workers to absorb great ideas. Yet she was also more than willing to give time to a backward village boy who needed help with his arithmetic. Thibon speaks of her 'educative genius' and describes how she used to expound Plato to him in the evenings after the day's work. They also studied the Lord's Prayer in Greek together. Simone committed it to memory and made a habit of repeating the Greek words each morning until she had given them her full attention. The fruit of that attention can be seen in her meditation on the 'Our Father' published in *Waiting on God*.

Later in the year, Simone worked at the grape harvest and always refused to do less than the 'sturdy peasants' for whom, of course, the physical effort was far easier. She told Thibon that she found herself wondering 'whether hell did not consist of working eternally in a vineyard'.

Simone returned to Marseilles for the winter months. She expounded Pythagoras to a discussion group arranged by Fr Perrin, and she wrote a number of articles for the magazine *Cahiers du Sud* under the pseudonym 'Emile Novis', an anagram of her name which she used because her name was Jewish. Simone's arrival in the south of France had intensified her already awakened interest in the history of that part of the country,[15] and she began to study in detail a period which was highly congenial to her admittedly rather wayward historical judgment. It was that of the civilization of Languedoc and the Albigensian heresy. *Cahiers du Sud* published two essays by her on this subject.[16]

These essays represent a continuation and further exposition of the ideas which Simone had set out in her earlier pieces on the Iliad and the Roman Empire, and in her play *Venice Preserved*. The theme of the essays is the destruction of Greek and Christian values by collective power. It was a theme of great importance in Simone Weil's thought – we could call it one of her obsessions – and her representation of it through the tragic story of Languedoc is worthy of fairly close attention. But first we must try to fill in some of the background.

The area of mediaeval France known as Languedoc was roughly bounded by the rivers Garonne and Rhône to the west and east, and by the lowest slopes of the Massif Central to the north and the Pyrenees to the south. The natural capital of the area was the ancient city of Toulouse, which became the centre of a mediaeval civilization of remarkable genius. The various peoples of the area had one thing in common: they all spoke the same language. It was the Romance language of Oc, and the country came to be called 'Occitania' or 'Languedoc' (it was not identical with the modern French province of that name created by Napoleon). Occitania was the gateway into France for all

78

who came from Spain. It had been crossed by Hannibal's armies, and later by the Visigoths and Saracens. By the eleventh century, however, western Europe had entered a more settled period of history. A flourishing trade and commerce brought Jews, Moslems, and Persians to the west. A sudden spirit of openness emerged. 'Cities began to break out of their narrow stone fortifications; what remained of the Roman roads were traversed and trodden yet more often by merchants and pilgrims. And there was – immediately – a great flowering of literature and the arts.'[17]

Hardly anywhere was this more striking than in the south of France. In Occitania there was a flowering of lyric poetry which expressed the ideals of courtly love soon to be carried by troubadours across the whole of Christendom. In the language of Oc, those values were called *Pretz* and *Paratge*. A man had *Pretz* (literally, 'price' or 'worth') when he was inspired by a high ideal, observable in his bearing and manners. *Paratge* was nobility, quality of birth, the knightly virtue of courtesy and chivalry, expressed above all by devotion to a woman. The love of the knight for his lady was the love of an ideal of beauty and perfection. He could not possess her, and his only reward was a smile or at the very most a kiss. 'Her look alone had the power to transform whatever it lighted on, while he had only to cast his eyes on her to feel a better man.'[18]

In the Occitanian cult of chivalry, Simone Weil immediately recognized a re-emergence of the values of ancient Greece and early Christianity which had virtually disappeared under the Roman Empire. The love of the mediaeval knight for his lady was love of an impossible ideal – the same thing as Platonic love, whose real object is the divine. Such love excludes force and possession. 'It is simply a patient attention towards the loved person and an appeal for that person's consent.'[19] The word for this consent is the 'merci' of chivalry, which is equivalent in meaning to the Christian word 'grace'. It conveys the love of God through the person loved. Human love in the chivalrous sense is one of the bridges between man and God.

The Occitanian renaissance had in common with Greek civilization a total repudiation of force. This, says Simone, reached its fulfilment in chivalrous love, although the Occitanians, like Homer, realized that force is almost absolutely supreme in the world. The ideal of Occitanian society was that of pure obedience based not on force but on personal fealty. This ideal, Simone believed, was present even in relationships between artisans, merchants, and nobles. 'To obey a man simply as a repository of collective power is to degrade oneself',[20] but to obey him out of personal devotion and with free consent is to express one's human dignity. Unhappily, but perhaps inevitably, the twelfth century also saw the emergence of a new form of collective power which destroyed the civilization of Languedoc – namely, the mediaeval Roman church.

The idealism and devotion of knightly chivalry found remarkable expression in the religion of Languedoc. The service offered by the knight to his lady was offered to the Virgin, and the ideal of purity predisposed many Occitanians to welcome the religious asceticism of the Cathars, who came as missionaries from the east about the time of the second crusade (1140–50). Catharism[21] was in effect a re-emergence of certain second- and third-century beliefs and practices which the church had condemned as heretical. These early heresies, subsumed under the titles 'Gnosticism' and 'Manicheism', were a combination of Platonic and Persian ideas with Christianity. They represented man's conviction that he belongs to another home, a home of beauty and perfection almost infinitely removed from this world of finitude and unreality which was considered to be 'the reckless or evil improvization of deficient angels'.[22] The problem of human life was that of finding the key to the lost kingdom of light, of escaping from the prison of the material flesh with its passions and lusts into the order of reality and truth. The Gnostic Christ was not incarnate and he did not die on the cross for man's redemption. He came in order to give men knowledge (*gnosis*) which would open the doors of the prison and liberate them into Paradise.

The Catharist men and women who came to Occitania were vowed to a totally ascetic way of life. They travelled in pairs, carrying the gospel of St John (which they valued more highly than the others) in a leather scrip. They never ate meat because they believed that it aroused carnal passions, and they condemned sexual intercourse in all circumstances since it might lead to the creation of more imprisoned souls in human bodies. They forbade all violence and all taking of oaths. They abandoned the Christian sacraments, replacing them by an initiatory sacrament of their own which they called the *Consolamentum*.

The Catharist faith spread rapidly in Occitania, so much so that when St Bernard visited the county of Toulouse he found the churches empty and there was no audience for his sermon.[23] Catharism was not a spiritual movement within the church: it was, rather, a rival church, with its own sacrament and ministry, its own way of living the Christian life. It represented a repudiation of a church which had become too attached to this world, too enmeshed in the wheels of power, too uncaring about the things of the spirit. In the land of *Pretz* and *Paratge*, people were tired of worldly priests and an official, politically-minded hierarchy. They were looking for a new salvation, and it was the austere but gentle Cathars who seemed to offer it.

It is not hard to see why Simone Weil should have found the Catharist faith congenial to her, though one cannot be certain how deeply she understood its theology. She says in her essay on 'The Romanesque Renaissance' that 'the Cathars seem to have carried spiritual freedom to the point of dispensing with all dogmas',[24] but that was certainly not the case. The Roman church had good grounds for condemning the Cathars as heretical, since it was clear that they maintained doctrines essentially similar to those of the Gnostics, which had been anathematized a thousand years before. Simone was perhaps inclined to accord an uncritical reception to anything that reminded her of her beloved Plato and to by-pass the results of the church's long debate with Greek philosophy.[25] What really attracted her, however, was the Catharist way of life. Its ascetic self-denial, its spirituality, its acceptance of martyrdom, and above all its rejection of force, were for Simone the supreme achievements of the Greek and Christian spirit. Not surprisingly, she viewed the extirpation of the Albigensian heresy (as Catharism came to be called) as an unmitigated disaster, as yet another example of the triumph of collective power over the freedom of the spirit.

The story of the Albigensian Crusade mounted against the Cathars of Occitania by Pope Innocent III does not make pleasant reading. For ten years the Pope sent missions to Occitania, the aim of which was to bring the people back to the Catholic faith. They were totally unsuccessful, and ended with the murder of a papal legate on 15 January 1208. Having attempted peaceful persuasion, Innocent had no choice except force. A French army was assembled which captured the town of Béziers and massacred its inhabitants to the last man. The fall of Carcassonne followed, and the conquered cities were offered to Simon de Montford who became leader of the crusade. He was an energetic and able commander, genuinely convinced that he was fighting for Christendom against the forces of Antichrist. There was heroism and a notable absence of cowardice on both sides, but the repudiation of violence by the most devout Catharists meant that defeat on the field was inevitable. But when the Lateran Council of 1215 handed over the conquered territory, including the city of Toulouse, to Simon de Montford, the conflict became political rather than religious and the people of the South rose to repel the invader from the land of *Pretz* and *Paratge*. But the country did not escape conquest. As Simone Weil says, *Pretz* and *Paratge* were fated to disappear, since when 'we have been brought up in an environment almost exclusively composed of profane values'.[26] We cannot, she concludes, apply the Occitanian inspiration to the present conditions of existence (presumably she meant that Hitler would not be defeated by a Catharist repudiation of force); nevertheless, 'in the measure that we contemplate the beauty of that age with attention and love, in that same measure its inspiration will come to us and will gradually make impossible at least some of the ignominies which constitute the air we breathe today'.[27]

Simone once remarked that it is always the victors who write history, and no doubt it is true that defeated causes are seldom represented justly. Her essays on Languedoc were an attempt to balance the judgment of the victors, and perhaps she was guilty of idealization and a tendency to attribute only nobility to the Cathars and only turpitude to the Catholics. Yet she was not mistaken in seeing in the crusade an epitome of the conflict between freedom and organization – a conflict which is probably endemic to all civilizations and all religions. She was also right in thinking that the most frequent loser in that conflict is freedom, though perhaps she underestimated the importance of organization for any society which has got beyond the stage of bucolic idealism. The Catholics were not wrong in their belief that mediaeval Christendom was worth preserving and that the traditional doctrines of the church were more likely to be true than false. The Cathars were not wrong in recalling men to a life of personal holiness and a renunciation of wordly ambition. There were men on each side who recognized the values in the other; but, as always, it was extremism that prevailed and Justice which fled from the winning camp.

On 17 May 1942, Simone and her parents left Marseilles for a refugee camp in Casablanca – the first stage of the journey to America. Simone's ultimate plan was to join the Free French in London, where she hoped to be given a mission in the occupied zone of France. One has the impression that she was winding up a period of her life. She gave her papers to Fr Perrin and Gustave Thibon, telling her two friends to use them as they wished. She went, she said, without thinking of her return. She spent her seventeen days in the refugee camp writing furiously. Fr Perrin tells us that she monopolized one of the few camp chairs, an action which was so unlike her that one must suppose that she felt herself under severe pressure to put her thoughts on paper while there was still time.

Simone's months in the south of France had been a fruitful period for her. In Fr Perrin and Gustave Thibon she had found two steadfast, understanding friends who, although they were not conscious of having moved her convictions in any way, had performed the more important function of providing the kind of audience which her speculations needed. She had also worked on the land and had absorbed the beauty of the Rhône valley. She had even attempted to bring about the removal of the commandant of a camp for Indo-Chinese workers in Marseilles. These men had been brought to France to help in the war effort, but now there was no work for them and they were living in appalling conditions without heat or light. Simone visited the camp and protested against the treatment of the men. It was not without reason that Gustave Thibon remarked that her outspokenness could have got her into serious trouble with the authorities. The old Simone who had taken up the cause of the unemployed in Le Puy ten years before was still very much alive, but Vichy France was a dangerous place for a protesting Jewess. It was as well that she left, though she hated the thought that she might be running away. But she would never have gone if she had known that her hope of working with the Resistance would come to nothing.

NOTES

1. SG pp. 11–42.
2. ET 'The Great Beast' in SE pp. 89–144.
3. SE pp. 91–2.
4. SL pp. 145–53.
5. SW's play 'Venise sauvée' is reprinted in P.
6. JMP p. 15.
7. JMP pp. 8–9.
8. GT p. viii.
9. PT p. 116.
10. GT p. viii.
11. EWFT p. 14.
12. GT p. x.
13. See Introduction to CO by Albertine Thévenon.
14. GT p. x.
15. See SW's letter to Déodat Roché dated 23 Jan. 1941 in SL pp. 129–31.
16. SE pp. 35–54.
17. Jacques Madaule, *The Albigensian Crusade*, Burns & Oates 1967, p. 11. I am much indebted to Madaule's book.
18. Madaule p. 15.
19. SE p. 50.
20. SE p. 51.
21. The name comes from the Greek word *katharsis* (purification).
22. A phrase of J. L. Borges.
23. Madaule p. 34.
24. SE p. 52.

25. H. Chadwick (*The Early Church*) refers to second-century Gnosticism as 'an immense problem and threat to the Church', the most serious of all the early heresies.
26. SE p. 53.
27. SE p. 54.

7   In America and England

Simone and her parents arrived in New York in the second week of July 1942. They obtained an apartment on Riverside Drive overlooking the Hudson. Simone at once set about obtaining a passage to England. She wrote letters of heart-rending appeal to Maurice Schumann who had been a fellow student at the lycée Henri IV and was now in a position of importance with the Free French in London. She sent him her memorandum on front-line nurses which she had written before the French armistice, presumably with the intention of showing him that women could still perform valuable service in the most exposed areas of Resistance action. Simone herself pleaded for a job which would be dangerous, calling if necessary for death, though she admitted that her practical qualifications were almost nil. 'I beseech you', she wrote, 'to get for me, if you can, the amount of hardship and danger which can save me from being wasted by sterile chagrin. In my present situation I cannot live. It very nearly makes me despair.'[1] Her determination to return to Europe reminds one of the similar determination a few years earlier of another refugee from Hitler – the German theologian Dietrich Bonhoeffer. Both of them found unbearable the thought of being absent from the conflict with totalitarianism, and both of them, though in different ways, were to die as a result of it.

Schumann replied sympathetically to Simone's plea, and in November she at last obtained her longed-for passage.

In the meantime, she was filling her notebooks with an immense variety of material, and was, characteristically, studying the cultures of the Red Indians and American Negroes. She ventured into Harlem, the Negro area of New York, and attended a number of services at a Revivalist church there. She was especially moved by the singing. Although she frequented Mass, she felt more strongly than ever that she ought to remain outside the church. A letter written about this time to an old college friend, Jean Wahl, expressed some of her theological views in extreme form.[2] She detects 'one identical thought' in the ancient writings of Greece and Egypt, in Hinduism, Chinese Taoism, Christian dogmas, St John of the Cross, and the Cathar and Manichean traditions. She denies all originality to the Old Testament, claiming that the good things in it (Job, Psalms, and some of the prophetic writings) were derived from foreign influences. Almost all the rest of the Old Testament, she adds, 'is a tissue of horrors'. She thinks that Ham's observation of Noah's nakedness (Genesis 9.20–22) symbolized 'the revelation of mystical thought' which persisted among his descendents but was almost destroyed by 'the will to domination' which culminated in the Roman Empire.[3] These perverse judgments are in part consistent with Simone Weil's admirable universalism, her refusal to accept the boundary lines drawn between truth and falsity by narrow dogmatisms. This refusal, however, undoubtedly led her into dogmatisms of her own which caused her to polarize history into a kind of Gnostic conflict between the powers of light and the powers of darkness. To Simone, the Roman Catholic church (at least in its organizational aspect) belonged fairly firmly to the latter category, and although she thought that its dogmas and sacraments were genuine bridges to God, she did not consider that as such they were superior to Greek science.

In attempting to understand her more aberrant views, perhaps one has to bear in mind two important points. First, Simone felt that her vocation was to those who were *outside* the church, and she therefore looked for bridges to God which were accessible without prior commitment to the Christian faith. In her letter to Jean Wahl she remarks, significantly, that the truth 'requires to be expressed through the only approximately good thing we can call our own, namely science'. Some of her own most illuminating work was an attempt to do precisely that. Second, as T. S. Eliot reminds us, she died young, before she had been able to revise and order her ideas in the light of mature reflection. 'We should not criticize her philosophy at thirty-three as if it were that of a person twenty or thirty years older';[4] and perhaps also we should be glad that her passions so often compel us to think in wider terms than our own orthodoxies usually allow.

On arrival in England, Simone was sent for screening to an internment camp. She said in a letter to her parents that she did not mind this because it was a normal precaution. She was in the camp for nineteen days, apparently because the British authorities were doubtful about her communist leanings and her part in the Spanish civil war. Maurice Schumann got her released. She was billetted in a barracks in London used by the Free French until she found lodgings in Holland Park, where she was looked after by a widow with two children. As a lodger, Simone was no trouble except that she often refused food (she was determined to eat no more than the rations in France) and would not allow her landlady to clean her shoes. She told nursery stories to the little boy and arranged for a doctor to see him because she thought he might have a thyroid deficiency, which proved to be correct.

During the day, Simone worked at the offices of the Free

French. She was given 'intellectual work' to do, which included the writing of comments on political reports from the Resistance in France. Her 'magnum opus', however, was a blue-print for post-war reconstruction entitled 'Prelude to a Declaration of Duties towards Mankind' (later published as 'L'Enracinement' in France and 'The Need for Roots' in England). Whoever it was among the Free French who suggested that Simone should do this could hardly have had a better idea for her. The job itself was greatly worth doing and Simone Weil was uniquely qualified for it. But of course it was not at all what she wanted. Her whole being was set on getting to France and working with the Resistance. Again she turned to her friend Maurice Schumann, setting out in a long letter to him her imperative need to share in the dangers and, if need be, the torture and death, which awaited her in France. Simone seldom wrote about herself, and her letter is the more moving for that reason. She tries to show that the whole of her past life has been a kind of preparation for the mission she desires, that everything has converged towards this point as though it were her destiny.

> Although the thoughts which my pen transcribes are far above me, I adhere to them as what I believe to be the truth; and I think that I have been commanded by God to prove experimentally that they are not incompatible with an extreme form of action in war.[5]

The core of her argument is contained in these sentences:

> I feel an ever increasing sense of devastation, both in my intellect and in the centre of my heart, at my inability to think with truth at the same time about the affliction of men, the perfection of God, and the link between the two.
> I have the inner certainty that this truth, if it is ever granted to me, will only be revealed when I myself am physically in affliction, and in one of the extreme forms in which it exists at present.[6]

Simone Weil has been accused by some of harbouring a

secret death-wish. Charles Moeller remarks that if death did not exist, Simone Weil would have had to invent it. But her letter does not read like an irrational impulse towards self-immolation. It is, rather, entirely consistent with her religious awareness. As we have said, the centre of that awareness was occupied by the Passion of Christ and the affliction of the world. To be in one place when, as she said, Christ was being crucified in another, simply meant for Simone that there was no longer any reason for living. Her place was at the cross, and the cross at that moment of history was in France. That was why she wanted to go. There was no spurious heroism about it and no morbid desire for suffering as an end in itself. The Christ who had come down and taken possession of her had revealed to her only one way of obedience. There was and there could be no other.

But it was impossible for her request to be granted. No one could take the responsibility of sending her to certain death. Her Jewish appearance alone would have been enough to ensure her immediate arrest by the Gestapo, and her physical clumsiness and fragile health would have made her a doubtful asset to the Resistance. Her own contribution was to be the 'intellectual work' for which, to say the least, she was better fitted.

Although Simone often remarked in letters to her parents that her Free French colleagues were all 'very nice', she seems to have tolerated rather than enjoyed their company – with the exception of her friend Simone Deitz whom she had got to know in New York and who had also come to London. More and more Simone Weil seems to have retreated into herself, sometimes working so late at night that she missed the last tube and had to sleep in the office. There were perhaps three reasons for her withdrawal. She was carrying an almost insupportable load of disappointment;

she was doing an immense amount of thinking and writing; and her health was getting worse. Yet in spite of everything she enjoyed being in London. The spring of 1943 was an exceptionally fine one, and Simone often referred with delight to the blossom and flowers which were appearing in the parks and squares. She enjoyed a performance of *Twelfth Night*, and went to some of the Myra Hess lunch-time concerts at the National Gallery. She was 'enchanted' by the pubs in working-class districts (though she assured her parents that she did not enter them very often), and she spent hours on Sundays at Speakers' Corner, which she thought to be perhaps the only place in the world where the ancient Athenian tradition of open-air debate had been preserved. She found English food better than she had expected: she particularly mentions roast pork and apple sauce, though she is less enthusiastic about the English passion for jelly. She was impressed by cockney humour, and she thought that the police in England were 'something really delightful'.[7]

It was natural that Simone should have been thinking a good deal about 'patriotism' at this time. She admired England because she thought that the people there were less uprooted from their own past than was the case in France. The thing that had struck her most about *Twelfth Night* was the fact that Shakespeare's drinking scenes were similar to the atmosphere of present-day London pubs! Her principal theme in *The Need for Roots* is the importance of reconnecting the people to the values of their own history, of 're-rooting' them in the soil by which their nation has been nourished. In her diagnosis of the ills of the modern Nation–State (she is writing particularly about France), she discovers that the people live in their own country as if they were immigrants. They have been 'deracinated' from the earth by money-values and by the cold, impersonal power-system of the modern State. In familiar vein, Simone writes that the unification of France was accomplished by force, by a suppression of those local cultures which, in the Middle Ages, had given men tolerance, liberty, and a spiritual life. The Middle Ages had been an interval of freedom between the collapse of the Roman Empire and the re-emergence of Roman collectivism in the form of the modern State. The State has become an idol, a god, demanding of its subjects an absolute, unlimited devotion; and because men now have no other values in which to believe, they cling to the State as the sole repository of wealth and power. 'The State is a cold concern which cannot inspire love, but itself kills, suppresses everything that might be loved; so one is forced to love it, because there is nothing else. That is the moral torment to which all of us today are exposed.'[8]

Simone makes an important distinction between moral obligation which, in itself, is absolute and unconditional, and the specific objects in the world to which obligation attaches itself which are always temporary and relative. The only adequate object of moral obligation must itself be absolute and unconditional, and such an object is the individual human person, whose essential reality is grounded in a reality which is beyond the world altogether.[9] The human tragedy is that men give an absolute value to non-human objects of obligation in this world, and of these the State is the prime example. This leads not only to the slogan, 'My country, right or wrong', but even to the absurd belief that my country is always right.[10] Christians above all should have understood the difference between duty to God and duty to men, yet they have not only acquiesced in worship of the collective but have even created a powerful collective of their own. Moreover, Christianity now finds itself in an impossible dilemma in relation to secular life. Religion must either hand over the whole of secular life to the State and concern itself only with private options about the way in which to spend an hour or two on Sunday mornings; or else it must play the secular game and allow its ethos to be determined solely by the interests and values of the collective.[11] Yet it is equally wrong, Simone says, to abdicate from the world in favour of the Absolute, and to turn objects in the world into absolutes themselves. There is 'a spurious mysticism' and 'a spurious contemplation' on the one hand, and 'the lie propagated by idolatry' on the other.[12] But the proper function of religion 'is to suffuse with its light all secular life, public or private, without ever in any way dominating it' (that is, by the methods of power-politics).[13] 'It is only through things and individual beings on this earth that human love can penetrate to what lies beyond it.'[14]

There is a good deal in *The Need for Roots* which reminds one of that other religious thinker already mentioned in this chapter who was Simone's contemporary – Dietrich Bonhoeffer. His 'religionless Christianity' corresponds to Simone Weil's repudiation of the kind of 'spurious mysticism' which separates religion from the world, and his emphasis upon the need to speak of God 'in a secular fashion' corresponds to Simone's own conviction that love of God is attained only through love of man and the world. Neither Simone Weil nor Dietrich Bonhoeffer, however, lends support to the more extreme view of some 'secular' Christians today that the divine reality is itself limited to this world. Simone would have thought that such a conception was self-contradictory, since 'the supreme value' must necessarily transcend all other values, even though it finds 'implicit' expression in them.

How, then, can one love and serve one's country without idolatry? Simone lists four obstacles which must be re-

SCM BOOK CLUB

SCM Press Ltd · 56 Bloomsbury Street · London WC1B 3QX

A Happy New Year to All our Readers

Editor's Letter

With David Anderson's book on Simone Weil, the Book Club reaches its two hundredth issue and is still going strong. Members who have been with us from the start still write in to tell us so, and there is a steady inflow of new members to fill the gaps made by those who leave us.

I had hoped to have some small celebration at this time to mark the occasion, but the usual autumn rush and shortness of staff has proved too much. However, it may well prove possible to arrange something, at least for those members nearer London, when the comparative quietness and better weather of summer comes. As I look back over the two hundred books on the shelf in my room, they make an impressive collection, and one of the encouraging things is the way in which some of the names on the earlier titles have become familiar from later and more ambitious writings. It is amazing, too, how many of the club books are still on display on my other shelves, which house the books published by us that are still in print in other forms.

Do write and tell us how you are enjoying 'Six Christians' – and if you have any more ideas for new series or non-series, I shall be glad to know.

John Bowden

A Review by Norman Pittenger

*Norman Pittenger, a well-known and prolific author, is a Senior Member
of King's College, Cambridge*

As one reads David Anderson's fascinating account of the life and
thought of Simone Weil, one is reminded of the strange fact that
much of the world's advance, religiously as well as in other areas,
has been brought about by those whom E. W. F. Tomlin (quoted
by Anderson in this book) calls 'odd pieces'. In Christian history
there is an Augustine, a Joachim of Flora, a Luther, a Pascal, a
Kierkegaard. And now there is a Weil. Those who in various ways
are the 'odd man out' often penetrate more profoundly and tellingly
into the mystery of human existence – and of God – than the ordinary, devoutly orthodox, and conventional people.

Years ago, in conducting a seminar on Kierkegaard, I had
occasion to remark that while nothing much happened *to* him,
almost everything that can happen to a man happened *in* him.
Much the same can be said of Simone Weil, although her story –
from brilliant student to teacher, from socialist supporter of the
French trade-union movement to religious mystic, from factory
and farm worker to participant in the French Resistance Movement
during the Second World War – is not at all uneventful. Yet what
really mattered was not what happened to her but what happened
in her. In that respect she resembles Kierkegaard – and for another
reason too: nobody can read her, any more than he can read
S. K., and emerge the same person. These 'odd pieces' are like
catalytic agents; they change things for anyone who comes in
contact with them.

This book of David Anderson's, I venture to say, is a superb
example of appreciative biography and critical evaluation. Not
only is it written in a beautiful and lucid manner; it has the special
merit of making one want to read or re-read everything that his
subject wrote. There could be no higher praise than that. And
certainly Simone Weil is worth reading and re-reading – not be-

cause she will gain disciples but because she will provoke thought.

When a reading of George Herbert's poem 'Love' made Christ real to her — 'Christ himself came down and took possession of me,' she wrote — she may have been tempted to be baptized and become a practising Catholic (she was a Jew by birth, but not a practising one). Instead she remained outside the church. She reminds me of my old teacher Paul Elmer More who also refused to become a 'member' of the church since he felt, after his becoming a Christian, that he could do more to point the outsider to Christ if he did not become part of the ecclesiastical institution. She attended Mass; she prayed; she lived a life which was marked by self-abnegation, sometimes to absurd limits, since she wished to participate in the Passion of her Lord in his days of humiliation and agony. But she was highly critical of the church, especially the Roman Catholic branch of it, for its confusion (as she saw it) of faith with the wrong sort of dogmatism, its pretension to 'possess' the truth, and its intolerant and intolerable hierarchical and organizational structure.

For Simone Weil, Christian values were present in many non-Christian traditions, 'especially the Iliad, Plato, the mystery religions of Greece and Egypt, and the Bhagavad-Gita of Hinduism', to quote Anderson; but also in the Chinese Tao and in many other places, not least in the austerity and beauty of modern science. Hers was no secular theology but a theology of the secular: she was always 'passionately concerned about the world and its human afflictions' but she was equally passionate in her avowal of 'love at the centre of pain', and of 'a presence more personal, more certain, and more real than that of any human being' — in a word, of God as supremely and centrally the cosmic Lover.

A process-theologian may be pardoned for noting the Whiteheadian strain in her thinking, for her God is not sheer force but Love which works persuasively and with lure in the midst of the necessities of the world, himself suffering through identification with that world yet triumphant over its anguish because Love is indefatigable and indefeasible and subsumes pain in joy. There is a good deal in Simone Weil's thought that is doubtful, unorthodox, even wrong — as David Anderson correctly remarks. But the woman herself is *right*, in all her oddness and eccentricity going unerringly to the centre of things and making those who read her, or read about her, uncomfortable, ill-at-ease in Sion, discontent

with their simple solutions or cheap answers to enormously
difficult problems.

We owe a debt of gratitude to David Anderson for this fine book.
It deserves a very wide reading; but he himself, certainly, would
say that Simone Weil herself deserves an even wider reading. His
book is an invitation to do just this.

THIS MONTH'S AUTHOR

David Anderson

David Anderson went to school at the Royal Grammar School,
Newcastle upon Tyne, and from there to Selwyn College, Cambridge, where he was awarded an M.A. in English and theology.
The Second World War interrupted his training for the Anglican
ministry and after a spell in the Royal Artillery he went abroad to
serve as an intelligence officer in India, Burma and Siam. During
this period he became a qualified translator of Japanese.

On demobilization he went up to Wycliffe Hall, Oxford, and in
1949 was ordained to serve a curacy at St Gabriel's, Sunderland.
He returned to theological college life in 1952 as chaplain and
lecturer at St Aidan's, Birkenhead, and four years later went abroad
again as principal of Immanuel College, Ibadan, Nigeria. In 1962
he was appointed principal of Wycliffe Hall, a post from which he
resigned in 1969. He is now Senior Lecturer in R.E. at Wall Hall,
College, near Watford. Mr Anderson is married with three children
aged 15, 13 and 11. He is a great lover of music.

Printed in Great Britain by Billing & Sons Ltd., Guildford and London moved before true patriotism or 'rootedness' will become possible. They are our false sense of greatness, our degraded sense of justice, our idolization of money, and our lack of religious inspiration. Our feeling for our country should not be one of pride but of compassion. This will come when we recognize the fragility of all earthly beauty.

> The compassion felt for fragility is always associated with love for real beauty, because we are keenly conscious of the fact that the existence of really beautiful things ought to be assured for ever, and it is not.
> One can either love France for the glory which would seem to ensure for her a prolonged existence in time and space; or else one can love her as something which, being earthly, can be destroyed, and is all the more precious on that account.[15]

A love of this nature, says Simone, would be an open-eyed love which neither ignored the pure and genuine grandeur in the past nor blinded itself to injustices, cruelties, mistakes, falsehoods, crimes and scandals in the past and the present. 'Mankind's crimes did not diminish Christ's compassion. Thus compassion keeps both eyes open on both the good and the bad and finds in each sufficient reasons for loving.'[16] Compassion for our country thus leads to a desire that justice be done to all sections of society and that aspiration be turned from money-values to the cultural and spiritual values which collectivism has almost destroyed.

The Need for Roots is a long, tightly written book which resists easy summary. But it is well worth reading, if only to show, almost thirty years after its composition, how little its author's 'duties towards mankind' have been realized. The number of aggressive nationalisms has increased; the determination of human life by the cash-nexus seems more firmly settled than ever; more of our roots in the past have been torn up; propaganda is our daily diet, violence has become unexceptional, and the value of the human individual has been further depressed. It is a miserable catalogue, yet there are perhaps also a few things on the other side. In spite of some notorious exceptions, there is a little more social justice in the world, and the condition of the manual worker, at least in the western democracies, has greatly improved. Anyone who remembers the unemployment, the low wages and long hours of the 1920s and 30s must feel that days are better now. If anything, the pendulum may be swinging too far in the other direction – an inevitable result when labour is valued solely in terms of the money paid for it and industry and labour are organized in huge combines. Simone Weil's solution to this problem – to decentralize industry and to disperse factories into small, scattered workshops – is even less conceivable now than it was then. Another gain has been the achievement of independence by the former European colonies, which has happened far more quickly than even Simone Weil expected in 1943. She hoped that the colonies would retain their unsophisticated village life and would not set themselves up as nations in the European style;[17] but here she was perhaps guilty of the Rousseauist fallacy of 'the noble savage', and she certainly underestimated the political aspirations of what we have come to call 'the third world'. Not that she can be blamed for sharing in what was then a universal failure of foresight. Finally, our very misgivings as we contemplate the world we are creating may be a cause of hope. We are perhaps realizing that a civilization based on the maximizing of production and the maintenance of dividends is not likely to be worth living in. There are signs that this secular frame is beginning to crack and that human beings are again searching for a reality which matches the eternity in their hearts. In this situation, Simone Weil has a great deal to say to us.

Apart from some entries in her notebooks and a number of

letters to her parents, *The Need for Roots* was the last thing Simone Weil wrote. Jacques Cabaud tells us that one day she failed to arrive at the office, and her friend Simone Deitz found her prostrate on the floor of her lodgings.[18] A doctor was called who had her admitted to the Middlesex hospital in the middle of April. She was suffering from a lung condition, but it was not so serious as to preclude recovery. Simone, however, must have been one of the worst patients the hospital had ever had. She did not want medical intervention, and she ate almost nothing. She became so weak that she could not lift a spoon or fork and the nurse had to feed her like a child. She asked to see a priest, and received visits from Fr de Naurois, who had fairly recently arrived from France. Although she was now dying, the old argumentative Simone had not changed. She still refused baptism and argued with the priest in a style which he later described as 'highly abstract and abstruse . . . a thought that was elusive and at the same time prodigiously rich. . . .' Jacques Cabaud comments that she had reached 'a spiritual summit' where 'there was a certitude that she had known God, while at the lower level of her being a wonderful and very humble simplicity coexisted with an argumentative and disruptive intelligence'.[19]

Simone did not inform her parents of her illness, and when she was in hospital she continued to write to them from her Holland Park address. In spite of her physical weakness, her handwriting remained strong and clear.

She was transferred to the Grosvenor sanatorium, Ashford, Kent, on 17 August. The window opposite her bed looked out across the fields towards France. She died peacefully at 10.30 p.m. on 24 August, having as before refused to eat. While working in London she had limited herself to the rations in France, and in her weakened state her final refusal of food made recovery impossible. The death certificate attributed death to starvation, and an inquest was held which returned a verdict of 'suicide while the balance of the mind was disturbed'.

Simone was buried at Ashford. Seven people attended the funeral, including her landlady and French friends. In her notebooks she had once written:

> For the privilege of finding myself before death in a state perfectly similar to that of Christ when on the cross he said, 'My God, why hast thou forsaken me?' – for that privilege I would willingly renounce everything that is called Paradise.[20]

In her last letter to her parents, dated 16 August, Simone had said: 'Very little time or inspiration for letters now. They will be short, erratic, and far between.'

NOTES

1. SL p. 156.
2. SL pp. 157–61.
3. Compare SW's essay on 'The Three Sons of Noah' in WG pp. 177–91.
4. NR p. vii.
5. SL p. 171.
6. SL p. 178.
7. See SW's letters to her parents in SL.
8. NR p. 109.
9. NR pp. 3–9, 150–1.
10. NR p. 124.
11. NR pp. 113–14.
12. NR pp. 150–1.
13. NR p. 114.
14. NR p. 151.
15. NR p. 164.
16. NR p. 165.
17. SE p. 208.
18. JC p. 338.
19. JC p. 340.
20. CS p. 109.

98

8 Analogies

Simone Weil wrote a surprising amount during her short life. Although her ideas reveal a marked and even a perverse consistency, they do not offer us a fully worked out system of thought. They are contained in essays, articles, letters, and a large number of notes and jottings which she put down as they occurred to her. For the most part, her notes do not represent final judgments: they consist of ideas, stories, quotations, etc. which are in the nature of 'food for thought', to be chewed and ingested at a later time of leisure. Simone's ideas are therefore hard to summarize – quite apart from the fact that their range makes it impossible to survey them inclusively in a single view. She had a multifarious mind, and most of us today suffer from what she considered to be the general curse of modern thought – namely, the splitting up of knowledge into narrow specialisms which preclude any total vision. As we have said, Simone Weil was a great crosser of boundaries, and the greatest value of her thought may lie not so much in her treatment of particular themes (we have seen that some of her judgments were highly eccentric), as in her ability to detect relationships and correlations in ideas having little apparent connection with each other. This synthesizing power of her mind, as we have called it, comes out in her frequent use of *analogy*, the illumination of ideas in one field of experience by ideas drawn from another, apparently discrepant, field of experience. A study and exposition of some of Simone Weil's analogies may therefore be one of the most helpful ways into her thought.

We begin, where Simone herself began, with the widest discrepancy of all – the immense distance which separates God from the world. We may of course argue that this immense distance does not exist. We may say that the biblical God is one who communicates with men, who is involved in their historical existence, who from his own side closes the gap between himself and the world. Supremely, we may assert, the gap has been closed by the Incarnation, in which God 'took our nature upon him' and 'was found in fashion as a man'. That is all true, but it does not eliminate the immense distance. God is still in heaven and man upon the earth. God has not identified himself with man to a point at which he has ceased to be God. The immense distance has been bridged but it has not been eliminated. And as Simone Weil says, it is a mistake to think that one can live on bridges as though they were permanent habitations.

The question Simone seems to ask herself is, How can we think about, how can we represent to our minds, the nature of the bridge (or bridges) between God and the world? How is it possible for two such contrary conceptions to be brought into harmony with each other? One way of solving the problem must be ruled out. We cannot simply erase one of the contraries and leave the other as the sole definitive reality. We cannot, that is, fund the world entirely into God (monism), or fund God entirely into the world (pantheism). What we have to find is something which, against all rational expectation, belongs to both sides of the contradiction – something, that is, which *mediates* between the contraries, having, so to say, a foot in each camp. For Christianity, the mediator between God and the world is the Logos or 'Word' incarnate in Jesus Christ.

In this idea of Christ as the mediator, Simone Weil finds a relationship and an analogy between christology and Greek mathematics. 'Christ', she says 'recognized himself as Isaiah's man of sorrows and Messiah of the prophets – *and also* as being that mean proportion of which the Greeks had for centuries been thinking so intensely.'[1]

The 'mean proportion' of which the Greeks had been thinking was what we call the 'geometric mean'. Between any two numbers there is a third number which represents the ratio of the two numbers to each other. This third number is the geometric mean of the other two numbers, and it is found by taking the square-root of the product of the two numbers. Thus the geometric mean of 1 and 9 is $\sqrt{1 \times 9}$, which is 3. We can set out the ratio as $\frac{1}{3} = \frac{3}{9}$, which means '1 is to 3 as 3 is to 9'. It is easy to see that 3 is 3×1, and 9 is 3×3. The term common to both sides is 3, the geometric mean. It is therefore the 'mediator' between the two numbers, with a foot in each camp.

The problem which puzzled the Greeks was that some numbers have geometric means which cannot be expressed either as fractions or as whole or finite numbers (they are called 'incommensurables' or 'irrational numbers'). The geometric mean of 1 and 2, for example, is the square-root of 2, and it can easily be shown that no such number exists. If we try to work out the square-root of 2, we never come to the end of the decimal places. The Pythagoreans are supposed to have suppressed the discovery of incommensurables and even to have liquidated the man who made it, because it seemed to refute their fundamental principle that 'Everything is number'. But Simone Weil dismisses this legend as absurd. It was the Pythagoreans themselves, she thinks, who made the momentous discovery that, although incommensurable ratios like $\sqrt{2}$ cannot be exactly represented numerically, they *can* be represented geometrically.

The geometric method followed upon the discovery of the properties of similar triangles which had been made by the Egyptians.

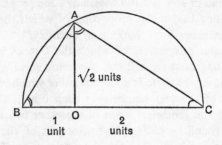

The base-line (BC) is divided into two sections (BO and OC) which represent the numbers whose geometric mean we wish to find. We take the arithmetic mean of the two numbers (that is, the centre of the base-line) and describe a semicircle whose diameter is BC. We then draw a perpendicular line (AO) from O until it meets the semicircle (A). This perpendicular line is the geometric mean of the two sections of the base-line (BO and OC). If, as in the diagram, the sections have the values 1 unit and 2 units, then the perpendicular will have the value $\sqrt{2}$ units.

For proof, all we have to do is to complete the right-angled triangle ABC. We can then show that the triangles BOA and AOC are similar, and therefore

$$\frac{BO}{AO} = \frac{AO}{OC}.$$

Simone Weil quotes Plato as saying that 'Geometry is the assimilation of numbers not naturally similar among themselves. Their assimilation becomes manifest when applied to the properties of plane figures, and this ... is a marvel which comes from God, not men.'[2] Simone adds:

Geometry offered (the Greeks) this marvel of mediation for the numbers which were naturally deprived of it.[3]

The notion of real number, arrived at by the mediation between any number and unity, was matter for just as clear demonstration as anything in their arithmetic, and at the same time incomprehensible to the imagination. This notion forces the mind to deal in exact terms with those relationships which it is incapable of representing to itself. Here is an admirable introduction to the mysteries of faith.[4]

Simone used the analogy of the geometric mean in a number of different ways. Just as the geometric mean mediates between two numbers whose ratio is numerically incommensurable, so also does Christ, the Word made flesh, mediate between the incommensurables of God and the world. Simone refers to the fairly numerous passages in the fourth gospel where Jesus represents himself as standing in relationship with God on the one hand, and with his disciples or the world on the other.[5] In short, Christ as it were represents himself as the proportional mean which harmonizes the contraries.

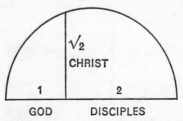

Simone takes the numbers which are incommensurable with unity as 'images of our misery', by which she means the misery of our own 'incommensurability' with God.[6] The Pythagoreans defined friendship as 'an equality made of harmony', and if we take 'harmony' in the sense of the geometric mean, remembering also that the only mediation between God and man is a being who is at once God and man, we pass directly 'from this Pythagorean equation to the marvellous precepts of St John'. It is by assimilation with the Christ, Simone continues, the Christ who is one with God, that the human being, lying in the depths of his misery, attains a sort of equality with God, an equality which is love.[7]

The analogy of the geometric mean can also be used in another way. As we have seen, the easiest method of representing a proportional mean between (say) unity and a number which is not a square is to draw a semicircle which determines its magnitude. Simone suggests that this semicircle as it were comes in from the 'outside' and 'transcends' the domain of numbers.[8] We can therefore take the semicircle as an analogue of God and say that Christ, as the proportional mean, harmonizes the contraries between man and man by his own determination with respect to God and man. What Simone means will become clear if we draw another diagram.

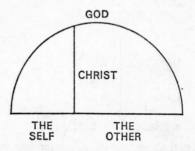

God and man are not the only 'incommensurables'. Man is also 'incommensurable' with man. Among men, says Simone, there is 'the brutal and mechanical character of subordination in relationships'. The reason for this is that 'everyone disposes of others as he disposes of inert things, either in fact, if he has the power, or in thought'.[9] Again, therefore, man needs a mediator, a proportional mean, who will unite the contraries – 'myself' and 'the other' – which are 'so distant that they have their unity only in God'. 'At whatever point in space and time two real friends are to be found, an extremely rare thing, the Christ is among them no matter what may be the name of the God whom they invoke. All true friendship comes from the Christ.'[10]

The analogy represented in the diagram above suggests God in Christ reconciling the world to himself and thereby reconciling man to his neighbour. This reconciliation, Simone says, involves the renunciation by man of the power to think of everything in the first person singular. God alone has the right to say 'I am'. That is his name and it is the name of no other being. 'The I am of God, which is real, differs infinitely from the illusory I am of men.' When man renounces his own illusory I am, 'he is granted the knowledge that other men are his fellows – before all, the weak and unfortunate neighbour whom, according to the laws of nature, we do not even notice in passing near him.'[11] It is through Christ, as the proportional mean, that we are united to God and thereby to other men in the harmony of friendship.

The analogy of the proportional or geometric mean leads Simone Weil to make the general assertion that God enters human life through the gaps in it. We must be careful not to confuse this idea with the 'God of the gaps' theory of our own time which has rightly been discredited.[12] Simone is not talking about gaps in our knowledge: she means the gaps between irreconcilable contraries, the gaps which are the point of entry of the proportional mean. These gaps are a kind of 'empty space' into which God can enter, but they disappear or become 'filled' when one of the terms of a contrary pair is eliminated. One example of this is what happens when the first person singular is renounced, not in favour of God, but in favour of the first person plural. We then create a collective ('We') in which the individual 'I' no longer has any significance. In such a case, it is impossible to create a harmony between 'I' and 'We' because there is no longer any distance between them. The 'I' has been funded into the 'We' and has virtually disappeared. Therefore there is no 'empty space' where God might enter, just as there is no geometric mean between a given number and zero. 'Nothing', says Simone, 'is more contrary to friendship than solidarity. The first person plural is not susceptible of being involved in a relationship of three terms of which the middle term is God. This trap for love is the most dangerous of all that are set here below. Innumerable Christians have fallen into it.'[13]

Simone Weil's idea that God enters human life through the gaps or empty spaces in it explains her rejection of all forms of 'consolation'. When we look for consolation, we are trying to fill the infinite gap between ourselves and God with something which is not God. Such consolations include things like money and material values, social status, various human ambitions and ideals which are treated as absolutes and are used to justify oppression and outrage. Even 'religion' itself is used as a consolation for the hardships and ills of our life here below, but when it is so used it is a bogus religion because it is an attempt to fill the infinite space between ourselves and God with something that is less than God. Only God can fill the infinite space, and we can only wait, in humility and attention, until he does so. We have to empty out from the infinite space its 'filling' of consolations and false absolutes. 'Affliction' is that experience of nihilation of the self which performs this work of emptying.[14] 'We must leave on one side the beliefs which fill up voids and sweeten what is bitter. The belief is immortality. The belief in the utility of sin. . . . The belief in the providential ordering of events – in short, the 'consolations' which are ordinarily sought in religion.'[15] In a letter to her friend Joë Bousquet, who had been severely wounded in the First World War, Simone expressed this conviction even more strongly:

> I am going to say something which is painful to think, more painful to say, and almost unbearably painful to say to those one loves. For anyone in affliction, evil can perhaps be defined as being everything that gives any consolation.[16]

This may seem a hard doctrine, but it is central to Simone Weil's religious experience and understanding. We may notice in passing that it refutes the theory of some that Simone was essentially a Gnostic. The Gnostics tried to fill the infinite space between God and the world by inter-polating a series of entities which were not God, which were less than God. But only the infinite God can fill an infinite space – or, to use Simone's analogy, only he can supply the proportional mean which harmonizes the incommensur-ables. Simone believed that God had done this in the crucified Christ, in whom the infinite distance of man from God was perfectly harmonized with the indivisible unity of God with God. Our own marvellous privilege is to be identified with Christ on the cross and to share in that harmony. 'Consolations' are, precisely, the things which keep us away from the cross and therefore from God.

The greater the distance between the contrary terms, the more astonishing is the achievement of the proportional mean which harmonizes them. Simone uses this fact in her understanding of the Trinity. There is a separation between the First and Second Persons of the Trinity, but this separation becomes infinite when Jesus, nailed to the cross, utters the eternal cry, 'My God, my God, why hast thou forsaken me?' At this point, Jesus has become identified with 'inert matter' which is as far removed from God as anything can be. His death, like the death of a slave, has been brutal to the point of making him 'a thing'. 'But', says Simone Weil, 'if this slave is God, if he is the Second Person of the Trinity, if he is united to the First Person by the divine bond which is the Third Person, one has the perfection of harmony as the Pythagoreans conceived it, harmony in which is found the maximum distance and the maximum unity between the contraries.' The moment at which the Son emits the cry of dereliction is therefore 'the incomprehensible perfection of love'.[17] 'God is not perfect except as Trinity, and the love which constitutes the Trinity finds its perfect expression only in the cross.'[18] Thus, 'the supreme mediation is that of the Holy Spirit uniting through infinite distance the divine Father to the equally divine Son, but emptied of his divinity and nailed to a point in space and time'.[19]

Those who have wondered what the Holy Spirit was doing at the hour of the crucifixion have here an answer.

Simone Weil says that the famous inscription over the entrance to Plato's academy in Athens, 'Let no one enter who is not a geometer', was 'an enigmatic affirmation of "No one cometh to the Father except by me" '. She also says that 'the appearance of geometry in Greece is the most dazzling of all the prophecies which foretold the Christ'.[20] Those of us, however, who are not geometers, even in the most rudimentary sense, may feel more like exclaiming, with Alexander Pope,

> See mystery to mathematics fly!
> In vain! they gaze, turn giddy, rave, and die.[21]

Even those of us who *are* geometers may agree with Pope's sentiment. The question whether mathematical models give us knowledge of the objective 'essences' of things, or whether they are no more than calculating instruments invented by our own minds, is one which has been a subject of debate since the time of Galileo.[22] What can at least be said is that, even if mathematics has no 'mystical' overtones, it undoubtedly contains a strongly 'aesthetic' quality which comes out in such expressions as 'a neat proof' and 'an elegant theorem'. Mathematicians have been known to prefer one theorem to another simply because of its greater aesthetic appeal. Simone Weil regretted that the mathematical mysticism of the Pythagoreans and Plato had been lost in modern times. She thought that 'authentic, rigorous certainty concerning the incomprehensible mysteries' was 'the infinitely precious use of mathematics ... one of the gaps through which real Christianity may once again filter into the modern world'.[23] In fact, however, Simone's theological use of mathematical analogies will probably stand up even without acceptance of the 'mystical' view, since the domains between which an analogy is drawn do not have to be true in the same kind of way for the analogy to work. We shall return to this point later.

Simone Weil did not think that her analogies were suitable only for the enlightenment of a small, intellectual élite. In her essay entitled 'Condition Première d'un Travail Non Servile', which she wrote in 1941, she suggested that factory workers be taught the mechanical laws derived from geometry by which machines are governed.[24] Such knowledge, she thought, would enable workers to see their machines as intermediaries between themselves and God. 'Only one thing can make monotony supportable, and that is a light of eternity, that is beauty.' The source of this beauty is God, but intermediaries are needed. Where can such intermediaries be found in factory life? One cannot stick up religious pictures! But circular and alternating movement presents an image of God and of man's relationship to him. Circular movement symbolizes the eternal, changeless act of God, oriented towards itself and with no other object except itself. Alternating movement, however, symbolizes man's 'covetousness', the movement oriented away from its origin until it reaches the limit of its travel when it changes direction and thus is forced to oscillate. This oscillation, says Simone, 'is a degraded reflection of the orientation towards itself which is exclusively divine'. The two kinds of movement are combined in 'the simple spectacle' of a pulley. Simone seems to mean that man always tries to move away from his true identity in God, but is halted by limits which force him back in the opposite direction, thus setting up a kind of alternating movement like that of a piston. The 'limits' are set by the circular movement of the crankshaft, which is itself an image of God. These truths, says Simone, and many others like them, can be read by means of very elementary knowledge of geometry. As we have seen, Simone believed that man's free consent to 'necessity' or 'limits' was an act of self-renunciation which opened the way to the vision of God. The mechanical limits of alternating movement offer us a kind of image or parable of this renunciation.

We may feel that Simone's mechanical analogy is another example of her tendency to over-estimate the intellectual capacity of ordinary, untrained people. Her 'model' is by no means easy to grasp, though of course in her essay she was setting it out in brief outline and with a minimum of explanation. We may, indeed, have misunderstood the way in which she meant it. Perhaps not many people would find in it the intuition of divine truth which was evident to a Simone Weil. But who knows whether, with her 'educative genius', she might not have been able to convey something of that intuition to her factory workers?

Another of Simone's mechanical analogies is offered as an

'inspiration' (not, be it noted, as a 'consolation') to those who 'carry burdens, manipulate levers, are fatigued by the weight of things'. This analogy is between a balance and the cross of Christ. A balance will balance two unequal weights if one arm of the balance is proportionately longer than the other. The arm of the 'balance' on which Christ is suspended reaches from earth to heaven; therefore, although his body is light, it counterbalances the universe. 'He who fastens on to heaven can do the same.'[25]

A favourite analogy of Simone Weil is found in the growth of plants. The astonishing thing about growth is that it is a defiance of the universal law of gravity. Simone takes gravity itself as an analogue of the pull away from God in the moral and spiritual order. Again we find her doctrine of the reconciliation of contraries. God, as it were, diminished himself in his creation of the world; he deliberately renounced direct control over it and even built into the world a force which always seeks to extend the distance of the world away from himself. This force is 'gravity' and its counterpart which is human sin. But there is also another form of energy which overcomes the pull of 'gravity'. The light of the sun creates chlorophyll which enables a plant to grow upwards. This light is an analogue in the material order of the operation of divine grace in the moral and spiritual order. Grace comes to us from outside, from God, and enables us to grow towards him, thus defying the 'gravity' which pulls us in the opposite direction. Solar energy is therefore an image of Christ, who came down to us in order that we might feed on the creative spiritual light. Just as solar energy enters our bodies through bread, wine, oil, fruit, so also spiritual energy enters our souls through Christ, who is himself 'the bread which came down from heaven'. 'The entire work of a peasant', says Simone, 'consists in tending and serving this vegetal virtue which is

111

a perfect image of Christ.'[26] In the same way as the energy of a machine can be an image of God to a factory worker, so the energy of growth and nutriment can be an image of God to a worker on the land.[27]

Analogies are always rather tricky things to handle. A particular analogy may 'work' for one person but be opaque or even ridiculous to another. One reason for this is that the two sides of an analogy never correspond to each other at all points, and sometimes the dissimilarity between them is so much more obtrusive than the similarity that the comparison appears grotesque. Simone Weil's analogy of 'the chicken and the egg' has struck some people in this way. It is an attempt to offer an 'image' of Paul's words, 'I live, yet not I, but Christ lives in me.' God, says Simone, plants the seed of his word, which is Christ, into the human soul as a germ is planted in a fertilized egg. Christ then feeds on the soul, he 'devours' it, in the same way as the germ 'devours' the egg in the process of becoming a chicken. The soul is separated from reality by the 'shell' of egoism, subjectivity and illusion, but Christ breaks this shell just as the chicken breaks the egg, and the soul, which is now in him, emerges into the real world. Finally, the soul will develop 'wings' and will 'break the egg of the world and pass to the other side of the sky'.[28]

Charles Moeller comments on this analogy: 'No, Christ in us is not a parasite; our soul is not this receptacle of passive material. God is not this cancer which devours us.'[29] In place of the loving dialogue between the soul and God, he adds, the system of Simone Weil offers us nothing but monsters, robbers of liberty, and slaves. Simone said that the symbolic meaning of the egg should be explained to farmers' wives who raise chickens.[30] Moeller remarks, 'I do not know whether to laugh or cry.' This is, for Moeller, clearly a case where the dissimilarity between the terms of the analogy is so great that the analogy seems merely absurd, and the point of it is lost.

Perhaps we should also remind ourselves that an analogy does not *prove* anything. We cannot argue that because an analogue of something is true, therefore the thing of which it is an analogue is also true in the same kind of way. If we accept the old distinction between reason (*ratio*) and intuition (*intellectus*), we must say that analogy belongs to the latter kind of activity rather than the former. The function of analogy is comparable to that of the figurative use of language in poetry. When it 'works', it enables our minds to make a kind of leap from the familiar to the mysterious, from the known to the unknown, from what is extensive to what is intensive.[31] Simone Weil does not, of course, use analogies as rational 'proofs'. She was, after all, a professional philosopher, so she was not likely to make such an elementary logical blunder. But as one who belonged firmly to the Platonist tradition, she believed that 'intuitive attention' was 'the unique source of art which is perfectly beautiful, of scientific discoveries which are truly luminous and new, of philosophy which truly moves towards wisdom, of love of neighbour which is truly helpful; and when such attention is turned towards God, it constitutes true prayer'.[32] Her own use of analogies belonged to that 'intuitive attention' by which, as she believed, man could become accessible to the mystery of God. For those who developed this power of attention, the world could become transparent to the light of God, instead of being a thick, impenetrable screen. She once compared this to the difference between reading something the right way up and upside down. In the first case, we see through the printed words to their meaning; in the second case, we see nothing but a jumble of opaque, unintelligible marks. Her own vocation was to help people to read the world the right way up, and that

113

was why she wanted workers to understand the 'images of God' offered by mechanical and biological processes. That was also the reason for her blasts against modern scientific rationalism and the whole humanist outlook which emerged at the Renaissance.[33] 'To find a place in the budget for the eternal', she remarked, 'is not in the spirit of our age.'[34] She distinguished between 'genius' and 'talent', the former being marked by 'the supernatural virtue of humility in the domain of thought', the latter by a pride which exalts personal achievement and never reaches 'the impersonal good'.[35] 'The difference between a more or less intelligent man', she wrote, in a memorable phrase, 'is like the difference between criminals condemned to life imprisonment in a smaller or larger cell. The intelligent man who is proud of his intelligence is like a condemned man who is proud of his large cell.'[36] The important thing is to come to the end of intelligence and pass beyond it to the domain of wisdom; and paradoxically, it is precisely modern science, in which twentieth-century man finds his greatest cause of intellectual pride, that can offer us, when studied with 'intuitive attention', the virtue of humility which pierces the screen between ourselves and the wisdom of God.

NOTES

1. IC p. 161.
2. IC p. 161.
3. IC p. 162.
4. IC p. 164.
5. John 10.14, 15; 15.9, 10; 17.11, 18, 21–23.
6. CO p. 269.
7. IC p. 171.
8. CO p. 269.
9. IC p. 173.
10. IC p. 177.
11. IC p. 175.
12. This is the view that God must be brought into our scientific account of the world in order to fill the gaps in our knowledge. Clearly,

as our knowledge increases God is gradually squeezed out. But God must be the God of our knowledge as well as our ignorance.

13. IC p. 177.
14. IC pp. 198–9.
15. GG p. 13.
16. SL p. 142.
17. IC p. 169.
18. IC p. 170.
19. IC p. 197.
20. IC p. 171.
21. *The Dunciad*, Bk IV, lines 647–8.
22. There is a good account of this debate, and also of the influence of incommensurables on Plato's philosophy, in K. R. Popper, *Conjectures and Refutations*, Routledge & Kegan Paul 1963.
23. IC p. 165.
24. CO pp. 268–9.
25. CO p. 263, cf. GG p. 85.
26. CO p. 268.
27. NR p. 83.
28. CS p. 253.
29. CM p. 253.
30. CS p. 254.
31. Compare I. T. Ramsey's 'cosmic disclosure' in *Religious Language*, SCM Press 1957.
32. IC pp. 269–70.
33. See the essays on science in SNLG.
34. SNLG p. 70.
35. SE pp. 24–5.
36. SE p. 26.

Postscript

J. L. Borges has a story in which a modern French scholar named Menard composes a version of Don Quixote which is word for word *identical with the original Spanish*.[1] It is not a transcription of the seventeenth century work but a recreation of it by a man who lived three hundred years later. Although the second Don Quixote is verbally identical with the first, however, it is 'almost infinitely richer'. One reader detects in it the influence of Nietzsche; another finds a sentence which, though a mere rhetorical phrase in Cervantes' version, becomes in that of Menard an astounding definition of history; another finds expressions which are 'brazenly pragmatic' in the style of William James. Borges' point is, of course, that we never read the masterpieces of the past as their authors intended them to be read. We write our own Quixote, our own Hamlet, our own Antigone. Our versions are word for word the same, but the meanings are twentieth-century meanings.

One almost has the impression that Simone Weil, in the manner of Borges' French scholar, was creating Christianity independently, without reference to the 'original'. Of course that statement, to say the least, is an exaggeration. We are not suggesting that she did not read and study the gospel or that she wilfully distorted it. What is quite certain, however, is that she thought everything out afresh and owed very little indeed to other interpreters, either ancient or modern. Such theologians as she had read – Augustine, Aquinas,

116

Pascal, Maritain – she was inclined to dismiss as wrong-headed. One result of this independence was, as we have noticed, a bias towards Gnostic types of speculation and a somewhat unbalanced assessment of Jewish and Christian history. But the overall gain was enormous. Every word that she wrote was real to her, everything had passed through the fire of her own life, none of it was second-hand opinion or fashionable judgment. When Simone Weil wrote about the crucifixion, she was not reflecting upon a theological doctrine: she was objectifying and transcending the affliction of her own soul and body. When she wrote about the harmonization of contraries, she was not playing with an interesting idea: she was describing the miracle by which Christ had crossed the infinite space and come to possess her. When she wrote about the brutal necessity of the world, she was not indulging in a safely distanced charity: she was expressing the condition of those whose servitude she had shared. And because she was 'a child of our time' for whom the puzzles and ignominies of the twentieth century were terribly and devastatingly real, she was able to create 'a new sanctity', as she called it, which is a possible religion for modern man because it encompasses both his achievements and his despairs. To use a metaphor which might have appealed to her, she was a free-range hen, not a battery one, and the food she offers us has a richer flavour than that produced by the batteries of orthodoxy. Perhaps one may regret that she never exchanged ideas with those who were her theological and philosophical equals. In particular, one thinks of N. A. Berdyaev, the great Russian theologian who lived in Paris and whose own intellectual pilgrimage had been not unlike that of Simone Weil. But they never met, and Simone does not seem to have read any of his books, though she would have found his ideas about the freedom of the Spirit, for example, and his hatred of

117

collectivism very similar to her own. Yet in the end one cannot wish her to have been other than she was – a 'pilgrim of the absolute' whose vision pierces the shell of the world and enables us, across the limits and afflictions of our finitude, to see the light of God.

NOTE

1. J. L. Borges, 'Pierre Menard, Author of the Quixote' in *Labyrinths*, Penguin 1970.

Index of Names

Weil, Simone,
  'The Love of God and Affliction', 61
  'Forms of the Implicit Love of God', 65–6
  Essays on the Iliad and the origins of Hitlerism, 70–2
  front-line nurses, 72, 87
  Venice Preserved, 73
  in Marseilles; meets Fr Perrin, 74
  meets G. Thibon; works on land, 75–7
  Essays on Languedoc, 78–84
  leaves Marseilles, 84–5
  in New York, 87–9
  in London, 89–97
  letter to M. Schumann, 90–1
  enjoys London, 92
  The Need for Roots, 92–6
  illness and death, 97–8
  use of analogy, 99–114
  'intuitive attention', 113
  'genius' and 'talent', 114
  theological independence, 116–18